15

# Rigoletto

## Giuseppe Verdi

*Opera Guide Series Editor: Nicholas John*

*Published in association with English National Opera and The Royal Opera*

782.12

John Calder · London
Riverrun Press · New York

First published in Great Britain, 1982, by
John Calder (Publishers) Ltd, 18 Brewer Street,
London W1R 4AS

and

First published in U.S.A., 1982, by
Riverrun Press Inc.,
175 Fifth Avenue
New York, NY 10010

BRITISH LIBRARY CATALOGUING IN PUBLICATION DATA
Verdi, Giuseppe
 Rigoletto. — (Opera guide; 15)
 1. Verdi, Giuseppe   Rigoletto
 2. Operas — Librettos
 I. Title   II. John, Nicholas   III. Piave, Francesco Maria   IV. Series
 782.1′092′4        ML.410.V4
 ISBN 0 7145 3939 2

SUBSIDISED BY THE
Arts Council
OF GREAT BRITAIN

John Calder (Publishers) Ltd, English National Opera and
The Royal Opera House, Covent Garden Ltd receive financial
assistance from the Arts Council of Great Britain. English
National Opera also receives financial assistance from the
Greater London Council.

Typeset in Plantin by Margaret Spooner Typesetting, Dorchester, Dorset.

Printed and bound in Great Britain by Whitstable Litho Ltd., Whitstable, Kent.

# Opera Guide

## Rigoletto

### Verdi

*Titta Ruffo as Rigoletto. Ruffo never sang the role at Covent Garden although he was billed to do so in 1903. He was so successful at the public dress rehearsal that Melba, who was to sing Gilda, protested that he was too young to sing her father, and he was removed from the cast. He sang regularly at La Scala, and at the Met. from 1921 to 1929. (Teatro alla Scala)*

# Preface

This series, published under the auspices of English National Opera and The Royal Opera, aims to prepare audiences to enjoy and evaluate opera performances. Each book contains the complete text, set out in the original language together with a current performing translation. The accompanying essays have been commissioned as general introductions to aspects of interest in each work. As many illustrations and musical examples as possible have been included because the sound and spectacle of opera are clearly central to any sympathetic appreciation of it. We hope that, as companions to the opera should be, they are well-informed, witty and attractive.

Nicholas John
Series Editor

# Contents

# List of Illustrations

# Introduction

*Jonathan Keates*

The première of *Rigoletto* at the Teatro La Fenice in Venice in 1851 took place in a city still bitter with the sense of humiliating surrender after the months of resistance to the siege which followed the heroic revolt against Austrian rule in 1848. No Italian community had so vigorously challenged the Hapsburg regime, and the extraordinary courage of the Venetians were a tribute to their deeply-ingrained sense of community. Despite attack from red-hot cannon balls, appalling food shortages and a severe cholera epidemic, the people had repeatedly answered their leaders with cries of 'No surrender' and their resilience became a byword in the annals of *Risorgimento* Italy.

Even had he chosen to do so, Verdi could scarcely have ignored the significance of Venice in the context of the cause of national unification he so fervently supported. Practically all his early operas feature in their texts some sort of challenge to orthodoxy, whether social or political, on the part of the principal characters, and many of their situations, however carefully swathed in the trappings of history, would have been instantly familiar to contemporary audiences. It requires little imagination to transform a figure like the defiant brigand Ernani, a renegade nobleman of impeccable lineage, into the young man of good family who was ready to take up arms against the Neapolitan Bourbons. *I Due Foscari*, arguably the gloomiest product of what Verdi called his *'anni di galera'* (galley years), offers the most poignantly characteristic of *risorgimentale* images — the hero's imprisonment and exile, his wife's tenacity and devotion on his behalf, and the aged doge's enforced retirement — which reflect the grimmest commonplaces of revolutionary experience in 19th century Italy.

It was therefore hardly mere coincidence that, from *Nabucco* (1842) onwards, his works took on a potent emblematic significance among Italian

*Raffaele Mirate and Felice Varesi who created the roles of the Duke and of Rigoletto in 1851.*

*Tito Gobbi at Covent Garden in 1956.*　　*Enrico Caruso as the Duke in 1902.*

audiences, and his unique, unmistakable voice, harsh and strident as it sometimes appeared to critics nurtured on Donizetti and Bellini, was readily identified with liberalism and dissent. In 1843 the poet Giuseppe Giusti, in a characteristic mixture of biting satire and rueful tenderness, described the experience of listening to the chorus *'Oh Signore del tetto natio'* from *I Lombardi* in the company of a party of Croat soldiers in Austrian employ. He watched fascinated as the soldiers closest to him became visibly moved by the music, and began to sing themselves.

> Silent and scorned, they stand alone, hemmed in by their tough military life and harsh discipline, blind instruments of a greed which is no concern of theirs, and which they know nothing about. And such mutual hatred between Lombard and Croat helps those who would divide and rule.

Practically every Verdi opera of the decade contained some element which could be seized upon by the politically inclined listener: the jubilation which greeted *Giovanna d'Arco* and *Macbeth* at their first performances, in 1845 and 1847 respectively, was strongly coloured by elements which had little to do with a purely musical enthusiasm. Giusti, himself, however disapproving of Verdi's choice of subject in *Macbeth*, warmly appreciated the universal quality of the music's appeal. 'The type of sorrow that now fills the hearts of us Italians', he wrote to the composer, 'is the sorrow of a people who feel the need of a better destiny; it is the sorrow of one who repents and awaits and longs for regeneration. My Verdi, accompany with your noble harmonies this lofty and solemn sorrow, do what you can to nourish it, to strengthen it, to direct it towards its goal.'

Verdi had certainly done this with his two previous operas for La Fenice. Unlike many other Italian theatres it was run by a committee of noblemen, chaired by a *Presidente agli Spettacoli*, all of them at that time ardent Verdians, and it is not difficult to see an oblique approval of all the composer stood for in the comment scribbled by the liberally-inclined Count Correr, mayor of Venice, on the proposal for an opera for the 1843-4 Carnival season: 'Verdi is necessary for every reason and is the only one I approve'. *Ernani*'s triumph, underwritten by the Venetian nobility, was echoed in other Italian cities and the ultimate revolutionary accolade was given when, two years later, an ecstatic chorus in Bologna, hailing the accession of Pius IX to the papal throne, turned the words acclaiming the Emperor Charles at the end of Act Three into *'A Pio Nono sia gloria ed onor'* ('Glory and honour to Pius IX'). A comparable popularity greeted Ezio's *'Arrai tu l'universo, resti l'Italia a me'* ('You may have the world as long as Italy remains to me') in *Attila*, produced at La Fenice in 1846.

It was during preparations for *Ernani* that Verdi first made the acquaintance of Francesco Maria Piave, the Venetian literary amateur whom the maestro, through a mixture of bullying and cajolery, transformed into the author of some of the most effective of his librettos. Piave had written texts for Mercadante and Pacini, and, though hardly an outstanding poet, he had, nevertheless, a powerful sense of theatre. On a purely personal level he seems to have been regarded, if not by Verdi himself, at any rate by Giuseppina Strepponi, the composer's mistress, as something of a mixed blessing: a good influence on Verdi's manners but a bad example in his continual philandering among Venetian women of every class. Their collaboration had already produced six lyric dramas, including *I Due Foscari*, *Attila* and *Macbeth*, by the time the composer signed his contract in April 1851 for a new opera for the carnival season the following year. 'I have in mind', Verdi wrote to him, 'a subject that would be one of the greatest creations of the modern theatre if only the police would allow it. Who knows? They allowed *Ernani*, they might even allow us to do this and at least there are no conspiracies in it. Have a try! The subject is grand, immense and there's a character in it who is one of the greatest creations that the theatre of all countries and all times can boast. The subject is *Le Roi s'amuse* . . .'

Verdi had contemplated an operatic treatment of Victor Hugo's sensational drama (based on an imaginary episode in the private life of Francis I of France) for at least six years before suggesting it to Piave. The play had itself been a distinguished victim of counter-revolutionary censorship in the Paris of 1832. The morning after its première the director of the Comédie-Française received a curt note from the Minister of Public Works ordering an instant suspension of all further performances. The piece was not revived for another fifty years, and has never since achieved the kind of classic status accorded to the same author's *Hernani* and *Ruy Blas*.

Reading *Le Roi s'amuse* for the first time we can scarcely fail to perceive the elements in it which must have appealed most strongly to Verdi. This highly-

*Paolo Silveri at Covent Garden in 1949*  *Riccardo Stracciari as Rigoletto in 1935*

9

charged story of Francis I's seduction of the daughter of his jester Triboulet was not just a contentious affair politically, but has other features bound to shock a respectable Parisian audience. The *Journal des Débats* voiced a typical conservative reaction when it exclaimed: 'Are these the sort of customs which art ought to expose to the public gaze? . . . In the classical theatre an exiled and unhappy royalty sought refuge on the slopes of Cithaeron leaning upon the arm of Antigone: on our modern stage, royalty slumbers drunkenly in a place of vulgar resort, embraced by a woman of the town. And this is what is called progress!' The composer must surely also have read Hugo's address before the tribunal to which he had fruitlessly appealed, a noble essay in rational indignation, and have noted, in the dramatist's defence of the play's essential morality, the words 'The real subject of the drama is *the curse of M. de Saint Vallier*' (Monterone in the opera), an idea which transferred itself easily enough, as a unifying factor, to the music. Verdians may also care to observe that Hugo compares his experiences with the censor to those of Desdemona smothered by Othello.

Piave's adaptation is amazingly faithful to the French text, transferring many of the most effective lines, such as :

> Sur le lion mourant vous lâchez votre chien!

or

> Courtisans! courtisans! démons! race damnée!

wholesale to the opera, and making only two serious cuts. The King's seduction of Blanche now takes place offstage, and Triboulet's hysterical lament over her body in the sack, amid a crowd of passers-by, including a surgeon who examines the corpse, is made in solitude. Both Verdi and Piave, however, must have been aware of the potential difficulties with the notoriously touchy Hapsburg censorship which the play and its author guaranteed, and to which neither composer nor librettist was a stranger. Much has been made of Verdi's problems with the censor, but in the case of such frankly inflammatory works as *Nabucco*, *I Lombardi* and *Attila* he seems to have been remarkably fortunate. It was only after 1848 that censorship in all the Italian states noticeably tightened its grip and Verdi was forced to make modifications to various features of his texts which the authorities in earlier years might have accepted more benignly; Leonora and the nuns in *Il Trovatore*, for instance, are permitted no obvious references to anything religious, though Cammarano's original words had mentioned the veil, the altar, heaven and penitence.

In the case of *Stiffelio*, on which Verdi and Piave were working when the *Rigoletto* project was first mooted, the censor dropped his bombshell on the libretto only a few days before the première at Trieste, insisting that the reading of the New Testament story of the woman taken in adultery, which forms the ethical climax of the drama, be removed from the final scene. Such a reaction must have acted as a warning to the musician and the poet and was typical of the overwhelming repressiveness of Austrian rule during this period. That *Rigoletto* was actually performed is a tribute to the foresight and tenacity not of Verdi alone, but of the Fenice management, represented by the president Marzari and the secretary Gugliemo Brenna, and even of the much-despised Piave himself.

Initial negotiations with Venice during the spring of 1850 were marked by the hard bargaining characteristic of the composer, who remained throughout his life the tough Emilian peasant haggling for a good market price. There were continuing worries about the women in the cast, particularly the proposed soprano Sanchioli, whom Verdi considered wholly unsuitable because of 'what she calls her Michelangelesque poses' (Piave was later to add

10

*Giovanni Mario as the Duke and Angiolina Bosco as Gilda in the 1853 Covent Garden production. (Raymond Mander and Joe Mitchenson Theatre Collection)*

that Verdi thought it would be impossible to get anything out of her as Gilda and that she would make the opera fail. Evidently she was just too monumental.) 'I was going over several subjects again when *Le Roi* came into my mind like a flash of lightning, an inpsiration, and I said . . . "Yes, by God, that would be a winner." So then, get the Prezidenza interested, turn Venice upside down and get the censor to permit this subject. What does it matter if it doesn't suit Sanchioli? If we had to take notice of that no more operas would get written . . . Singers who can by themselves ensure a success . . . like Malibran, Rubini, Lablache, etc. etc. don't exist any longer.'

As Piave got to work on the libretto, now provisionally entitled *La Maledizione*, nagging fears as to the drama's acceptability to the authorities began to unsettle Verdi. Was this factor, indeed, part of the allure for him of Hugo's play? As usual, he blamed Piave for assuring him that all was well and wrote to Marzari:

> trusting in his word, I got down to studying and thinking deeply about it, and the basic conception, the musical colouring were worked out in my mind . . . Signor Presidente, it is essential that you should find ways . . . to obtain permission for *Le Roi s'amuse*, and to find a *prima donna* (whether of the first rank or not) who suits me. If these obstacles cannot be overcome, I think it would be in the common interest to dissolve my contract . . .

Verdi's misgivings were, as it turned out, very well founded. On November 11, Marzari conveyed the official request from the Austrian Department of Public Order that the libretto be submitted for inspection. 'This request is occasioned by a rumour in circulation that the drama *Le Roi s'amuse* by Victor Hugo, from which Signor Piave draws his new work, has had an unfavourable reception both in Paris and Germany because of the depravity with which it is filled.' Attempts to expedite matters by harrying Piave were apparently in vain, even though Verdi concluded a letter to him at the end of the month by saying: '. . . it seems to me that this is a matter which should not continually be put aside, and *if I were the poet*, I would give it a great deal of attention, all the more so in that you will be largely responsible if it happens (and let's hope to

God it doesn't) that this drama is not permitted. Speak to the presidency: take the necessary steps; and do everything as quickly as possible . . .'

What Piave had in fact engineered was a holding operation dependent on discreet modifications to the text he now called *Il Duca di Vendome*, but Marzari's next letter to Verdi quashed this altogether, enclosing the ominous verdict from the Department of Public Order. 'His Excellency the Military Governor Cavalier de Gorzowski, with his esteemed dispatch of 26th inst. No. 731, has ordered me to inform the Noble Presidency that he deplored the fact that the poet Piave and the distinguished Maestro Verdi have chosen to demonstrate their talents in the repulsive immorality and obscene triviality of the plot of the libretto entitled *La Maledizione* . . . The aforesaid Excellency has thus seen fit to ban the performance absolutely . . .'

As the officer who had received the submission of Venice's revolutionary government on August 28, 1849, Gorzowski, his authority second only to the Emperor's, was hardly a man to be trifled with. Yet, ironically, it was his reaction which seems to have determined the future of *Rigoletto* as a feasible proposition for the Italian operatic stage. Piave, probably rather guilty for having temporised over the business of clearing the libretto with the censors, now hastened to alter some of the text's most obviously offensive features and though Verdi was singularly unimpressed with the result, and sent a curtly dismissive note to his librettist, practically cancelling all further communication between them, it was Marzari who made positive efforts to salvage the project by renewed appeals to the Director of Public Order. With the proviso that the place and time of the action be altered, it was agreed that the Duke could be a libertine and an absolute ruler, that the jester could be deformed, and that there was to be no objection as to his carrying the dying Gilda in a sack.

So serious had the whole issue become that it was thought necessary for Brenna and Piave to leave for Busseto immediately in order to discuss matters with the composer. Verdi's detailed instructions as to their visit contain at least one telling detail as to the political realities amid which they were all at work. 'I am sending my small carriage to bring you and Brenna to Busseto. The servant (Giacomo) will be on this side of the Po because he doesn't have a passport\*. So don't be annoyed at having to walk these few paces, crossing the Po by way of La Croce, where Giacomo will be on the bank. He will wait for you until ten o'clock tomorrow morning (Monday), so make sure you leave Cremona about eight o'clock. You know my house and now that my mother lives in your room I no longer have two free. If you want to put up with two beds in one room they can be made ready; if not, the inn, as you know, is only a short walk away.'

The resolution of fundamental problems as to *Rigoletto*'s narrative content did not necessarily guarantee its acceptance by the authorities. A libretto in Venice of the 1850s required approval from the theatre management, the mayor of the city and the police, and though Marzari was soon able to assure Verdi of the first two, Piave, who now faced the composer's customary barrage of ruthless technical criticism, was having to await the prolonged deliberations of the Department of Public Order, to which he apparently had to apply in person.

I again ask your pardon for not sending the lines because, I repeat, I don't consider them worthy to appear before you and hope to do some better ones which I will send off to you with all possible speed. Oh, this

---

\* The river Po marked the frontier between the Duchy of Parma and the Austrian province of Lombardy-Venetia.

*Rigoletto* will mark an epoch in my life! Let me persuade you that I am neither indolent nor lacking in enthusiasm, but that no man can do anything of value without Minerva's assent.

At the end of January, formal approval finally arrived. 'For the last five days', Piave wrote, 'I have been running around like the devil from the government to the police, to the Comando di Piazza, to the Presidenza, I assure you that by the time this is over I shall be a real athlete.' At the very last moment there was a bid from the censor Martello to make further alterations to the period and the setting, but two days later Piave could write 'TE DEUM LAUDAMUS! GLORIA IN EXCELSIS DEO! ALLELUJA ALLELUJA! Finally yesterday at three o'clock in the afternoon our *Rigoletto* returned to the Presidenza safe and sound without amputations or fractures'.

From then on, success was more or less assured. Piave booked rooms for Verdi at the Europa on the Grand Canal and saw to it that a piano, 'Camploy's best', was at his disposal. The composer afterwards praised 'the zeal and exceptional conscientiousness' of the cast in rehearsal and performance, and in this respect *Rigoletto* seems to have been particularly fortunate. Raffaele Mirate, the Duke, had earlier been enthusiastically compared by Piave to the popular lyric tenor Napoleone Moriani; Teresina Brambilla, the first Gilda, came from a well-known musical family (her four sisters were all singers) and was chosen by Verdi from among the Presidenza's suggestions, because 'she sings better and has more attack', and Felice Varesi, well known as a Donizetti specialist at the Vienna Kärntnerthor and the creator of Macbeth, was to make his mark as Rigoletto.

Just how Varesi succeeded on the first night was later recalled by his daughter Giulia:

How many times have I heard tell of the emotions of that Venetian première. My father, ashamed and timid in his ridiculous buffoon's costume, did not know how to pluck up courage to appear before the public, for he feared their derision; and at the very last moment, it was Verdi himself who, giving him a shove to get him on stage, made him stumble over the boards behind the scenes and flung him onto the stage, staggering all over the place. The audience thought this an inspiration for a buffoon's entry, and were enraptured . . .

This and other similarly unconventional features brought *Rigoletto* a guaranteed triumph. The critic of the *Gazetta di Venezia* wrote: 'An opera like this cannot be judged in one evening. — Yesterday we were almost overwhelmed by its originality; originality or rather strangeness in the choice of subject; originality in the music, in the style, even in the form of the pieces; and we did not comprehend it in its entirety . . . the skill of the orchestration is stupendous, wonderful: the orchestra speaks to you, weeps for you, transfuses passion. Never was the eloquence of sound more powerful'. Verdi himself, comparing it with *Ernani*, modestly noted that it was 'a somewhat more revolutionary opera, since it is newer and more recent, both in form and in style'.

Revolutionary it was indeed, but in a double sense which subtly reflects both Verdi's personal and political concerns. Much of the opera had been written against a background of domestic squabbling between the composer and his family and of the censure directed at his openly-maintained liaison with the soprano Giuseppina Strepponi (who, incidentally, had begged Piave to send Verdi back from Venice 'a little less of a bear') by the prudish citizens of Busseto. The intimacy of the drama in *Rigoletto*, with its strong emphasis on the relationship between parent and child and the element of clandestine romance which sends Gilda to her death, is not only linked with an increasing drift away from the crowded stages of pieces such as *I Lombardi* and *Giovanna D'Arco* towards the claustrophobic tensions of *Luisa Miller* and *Stiffelio*, but seems to echo and transmute some of Verdi's own experience during this period.

It is singularly ironic that the censors should have been at such pains to change the time and place of the action, for in certain significant respects no Verdi opera relates more tellingly to the atmosphere amid which it was conceived. By shifting the setting from France to Mantua and turning François I to an unnamed Duke, composer and librettist brought the story into a poignantly familiar local context. The libertines and triflers of the Renaissance had their counterparts among the Royal families of *Risorgimento* Italy, and audiences could trace easy parallels between Verdi's Duke and, say, the philandering Carlo Lodovico of Lucca, whose chief minister of state was an Irish jockey, or the Duke of Parma, Verdi's own sovereign, whose principal talent was for performing backward somersaults.

Just as interesting is the sense of place so vividly conveyed in the final act. This is Verdi's own countryside, the relentlessly flat, poplar-strewn landscape of the *Bassa Padana*, where the Po and its sluggish tributaries (beside one of which stands Maddalena's tumbledown tavern) roll between their huge, shelving banks. There is something eerie and haunting about these silent river margins which makes them as perfect a backdrop to the murder and treachery of Act Three in our own day as in the composer's. Such a quality is an intrinsic feature of *Rigoletto*'s universal appeal, enhanced, rather than dampened, by the assiduities of the censor.

*Dmitri Smirnoff, the great Russian tenor, as the Duke. (Stuart-Liff Collection)*

# The Music of 'Rigoletto'

## Roger Parker

Although specialists have argued convincingly that *Luisa Miller* (1849) initiates a 'second manner' in Verdi's operatic style — a renunciation of the 'epic' format seen in operas like *Nabucco* (1842), *Attila* (1846) and *La battaglia di Legnano* (1849) — most opera-goers would see *Rigoletto* as the essential turning point. At least as far as popular success is concerned, they are of course correct: revivals of Verdi operas before *Rigoletto*, even the most popular (*Nabucco, Ernani, Macbeth* and *Luisa Miller*), are always something of an event; after *Rigoletto*, almost all the works remain firmly in the standard repertoire of the world's opera houses. Indeed, the composer himself seems to have been aware that the opera was a special case. Before setting to work on the score, he wrote to his librettist Piave:

> Oh, *Le Roi s'amuse* is the greatest subject and perhaps the greatest drama of modern times. Triboulet [the original for Rigoletto] is a creation worthy of Shakespeare! ( . . . ) It is a subject which cannot fail ( . . . ) I was going over several subjects again when *Le Roi* came into my mind like a flash of lightning, an inspiration, and I said . . . 'Yes, by God, that would be a winner'.

Some years later, even after the successes of *Il trovatore* and *La traviata*, he still referred to *Rigoletto* as his 'best opera'.

Of course, *Rigoletto* and its 'creation worthy of Shakespeare' are by no means typical operatic subjects, and it is characteristic of Verdi that he immediately saw this originality in terms of unconventional operatic forms. Italian opera in the first half of the nineteenth century was a highly stylized medium: the drama was articulated largely through a number of 'closed forms', each of which aroused precise audience expectations. Most notable of these was the so-called *cavatina*, a two-part solo aria divided into a *cantabile* (usually slow and lyrical, displaying the singer's ability to sustain a beautiful line) and a *cabaletta* (faster and more forceful, in which the singer often displayed agility and dramatic power). Convention demanded that major characters be introduced by these *cavatinas*, which often meant that the first act of an opera would be little more than a succession of similarly structured show-pieces. Equally obligatory was the *concertato finale*, which traditionally occurred at the mid-point of the drama. This was a large-scale form in which chorus and principals would join together for an extended peroration to bring down the curtain; it may be imagined how much plot manipulation was often needed to accommodate this. *Rigoletto*, now regarded as a *locus classicus* of Italian opera, must in this respect have seemed highly innovatory to its early audiences. It conspicuously lacks those forms which were most common (there is no *concertato finale*, and the principal character has no *cavatina*, nor even a conventional aria of any kind) and in that, as well as in more obvious senses to be mentioned later, it breaks new ground.

But whatever the eventual outcome, Verdi's initial reasons for enthusiasm over Hugo's play may have changed slightly as the opera took shape. For example, in another early letter he states:

> The entire story is in that curse . . . An unhappy father who weeps over

15

his daughter's stolen honour, derided by a court jester whom the father curses, and this curse catches up with the jester in a terrifying manner; it seems to me moral and great, supremely great.

As matters turned out, this was something of an exaggeration. Plainly the idea of a 'pivotal' theme had considerable attractions for a composer anxious to liberate himself from traditional forms (both in the musical and the dramatic sense), but ultimately the 'curse' idea is central only to the First Act, where most of the musical and textual references occur. The aspect of Hugo's play which did remain important throughout, however, and which indeed grew in significance during the composition period, was its characterisation. Initially Verdi's interest focused on Rigoletto himself, and his ideas were much influenced by the *Preface* Hugo wrote to defend his play. Both in the French drama and the Italian opera the focus is the same: a physically and morally deformed protagonist, who is redeemed by his love for his daughter. Verdi's correspondence suggests that, from the start, he was as fascinated as Hugo was by this dichotomy. But, in fact, preservation of all the characters' dramatic integrity as conceived by Hugo was crucial: from that flowed their particular musical personalities which in turn conditioned the musical forms in which they appeared. The other principals of *Rigoletto* are equally unconventional: the ardent emotions of the tenor are superficial; the character of the heroine markedly matures as the action progresses. Verdi's faithful realisation of Hugo's challenging conceptions gives the opera a unique power.

\* \* \*

Even before the curtain rises, in the opening bars of the Prelude, we hear the 'curse' theme (or at least its most common version) sombrely announced in the brass and woodwind [8]. The emotional charge it can generate is immediately demonstrated as reiterated brass notes build to a strong climax of brief intensity before the music again subsides in a restrained final cadence. The curtain rises to the sound of the *banda*, a stage band which was traditionally scored on only 2 staves by the composer and which was a fairly common feature of pre-Verdi Italian opera. Although in 1851 the *banda* was somewhat anachronistic (Verdi had made prominent use of it in several of his early operas), here it fulfils a precise dramatic function. On the surface, the banal sequence of dance tunes [1, 2, 2a, 3, 4] merely creates the necessary festive atmosphere; on a deeper level, however, the very emptiness of the music is peculiarly apt for a Ducal court where the pursuit of pleasure is all-consuming.

After a brief conversation between the Duke and Borsa, the dance sequence is interrupted by the Duke's first aria, *'Questa o quella'* ('Every women is equally lovely') [5]. Though much performed outside its operatic context, the piece still retains its dramatic appropriateness if performed without too much ostentation; its swinging rhythm, strophic form and simple orchestration are of course perfectly suited to the Duke's shallow, cynical philosophy of love. Verdi does, however, allow himself at least one subtle touch of irony: on the words *'De' mariti il geloso furore'* (*literally*: 'The furious jealousy of husbands') a solo horn refers quietly and punningly to the cuckold's traditional headpiece.

A Minuet and Perigordino (the former remarkably similar to the minuet in the Act One finale of Mozart's *Don Giovanni*) are added to the list of dances, and we begin to realize that the placing of at least some of the individual tunes is by no means accidental. The stately, aristocratic Minuet underpins the Duke's attempt at courtly dalliance with Ceprano's wife while the third dance of the initial sequence [2a] becomes associated with Rigoletto, sounding after his first entrance and during his sinister conversation with the Duke. This last exchange leads to the first ensemble, in which the Duke's theme

[6] brings the musical action full circle, as it were, by repeating the basic shape of the first *banda* dance [1]. From this point the dramatic movement becomes faster and more impelling. Monterone's impressive entrance is countered by Rigoletto's ironic monologue, full of Iago-like string unisons and trills, as well as bursts of laughter from strings and wind. This in turn stimulates Monterone's curse, with its magnificent reiterated rhythm in the orchestral interpolations; and then comes the final ensemble, in which the courtiers' hushed terror [7] gives way to yet another version of the descending figure heard in [1] and [6]. With that final proof of the scene's compelling musical unity, the curtain falls for the first time.

The opening part of the second scene continues the predominantly ironic tone. After a subdued recollection of [8], the conversation between Rigoletto and Sparafucile is underpinned by an orchestral melody [9] for muted solo cello and double bass. The tension between this dark sonority and the melody's rather carefree lyricism superbly parallels the disparity between the matter-of-fact nature of the dialogue and its sinister subject; it comes as no surprise to find that Verdi's apparent ease of expression here cost him a good deal of work when he was sketching out the opera.* The duet is followed by Rigoletto's famous *'Pari siamo'* ('He's my equal'), the first of the protagonist's

* The *Rigoletto* sketchbook, published in facsimile by Carlo Gatti in 1941, is, so far, the only extended example in print of Verdi's sketch material. It thus constitutes an extremely valuable document, contributing both to our understanding of this particular opera, and to our appreciation of the composer's working methods.

*Gwyn Griffiths and Don Garrard in the 1968 Sadler's Wells production. (photo: Donald Southern)*

extended *arioso* sections. *Arioso*, best defined as a mixture of recitative and aria, having the flexibility of the former but the emotional charge of the latter, is Rigoletto's most characteristic formal mode of expression precisely because it allows such freedom and such intensity. *'Pari siamo'* is framed by repetitions of [8], and explores the entire gamut of Rigoletto's character: it is significant that, as his bitter invective against life at the Duke's court gives way to tender thoughts for his daughter, the words *'Ma in altr'uomo qui mi cangio'* (*literally*: 'But here I am transformed into another man') have a melodic line in which a completely new lyricism appears in the vocal writing.

A sudden burst from the full orchestra [10] introduces Gilda and initiates the first of three extended duets (one in each act) for father and daughter. This one has two main sections, both led off by Rigoletto. The first, *'Deh, non parlare al misero'* ('Ah, do not demand of one so sad') [11], contrasts the jester's lyrical, 'paternal' vein (heard just before in *'Ma al altr'uomo'*) with Gilda's breathless, 'sobbing' line. The second part, *'Ah! veglia, o donna'* ('Oh dear Giovanna, guard my daughter') [13], is dramatically interrupted as Rigoletto rushes off to investigate a noise off-stage (at which point the Duke makes his furtive entrance). When he resumes, he is joined by Gilda and the musical contrast is even greater, with Gilda's girlish charm portrayed in highly ornamental, exuberant figures.

When she thinks she is alone, Gilda's childlike personality is further revealed by the delightful (almost Tchaikovskian) music of *'Signor nè principe'*, with its delicate orchestral texture of *pizzicato* strings and its duet between voice and woodwind. The Duke's passionate interruption leads to another duet which, in spite of the change in male partner, in some senses resembles the preceding one: the Duke's simple, direct melodic line [14] — so different from that rather melancholy passion one expects from a Verdian tenor — eliciting further ornate responses from Gilda. If the hurried duet of

*Luiza Tetrazzini as Gilda. On a notorious occasion in Chicago, she finished her 'Caro nome' cadenza off pitch and the conductor, her brother-in-law Campanini, whom she had insulted as 'merely a conductor' took revenge by introducing a correctly pitched very loud chord to display her mistake. They never spoke or performed together again. (Stuart-Liff Collection)*

*Opposite: Left: Frieda Hempel as Gilda, a role she sang with great success at the Met. in the early years of the century.*

*Right: Amelita Galli-Curci as Gilda, the role in which she made her sensational Chicago debut in 1916. She finally sang the role at the Met. in 1921. (Stuart-Liff Collection)*

farewell [15] loses this focus of character, it makes up in sheer rhythmic sweep and energy what it lacks in subtlety.

Gilda's only aria in *Rigoletto*, the famous *'Caro nome'* ('Dearest name') [16], continues the impression of her character established in the duets. The two flutes, the tiny violin motif which punctuates each vocal phrase, and the subtle harmony of the coda all contribute to the delicacy of orchestral effect, over which Gilda's dreamy thoughts of her lover take vocal wing. Verdi insisted that it should not be merely a conventional show-piece of soprano virtuosity. As he wrote to the creator of the role: 'I don't see where agility comes into it ( . . . ) The tempo ought to be *Allegretto molto lento* [it is marked *Allegro moderato* in the score]. At a moderate pace and sung *sotto voce* it shouldn't give the slightest *difficulty*'. The opening and closing of *'Caro nome'* illustrate Verdi's gradual tendency during these years to blur the outlines of set pieces. At the beginning, Gilda's musings on her lover's name allow the music to modulate subtly from the key of the preceding number, while at the end, even more radically, the courtiers enter and comment on Gilda before her aria is formally complete.

The final scene of Act One is a pell-mell of dramatic action, with the hushed *staccato* chorus [17] a single fixed point. As so frequently with Verdi (one need think no further than the finale of *Il trovatore*), the end is precipitous in the extreme; but there is time for Rigoletto to recall once more the curse, and so set the musical as well as dramatic seal on this section of the opera.

\* \* \*

In defending his drama against the censor, Verdi at one point found it necessary to stress what he considered essential to the Duke's character: he

*The 1964 Covent Garden production by Franco Zeffirelli designed by Lila de Nobile. (photo: Houston Rogers)*

had to be an *absolute* ruler, and an 'utter libertine'. Given this, there would seem little if any leeway for a complex, multi-faceted musical personality and indeed, in comparison with Gilda and Rigoletto, the Duke does seem rather one-dimensional. Significantly, he has three important solo arias, each of which isolates him from the emotional core of the drama and makes his musical presence rather static and self-sufficient. There is no appreciable sense of development from *'Questa o quella'* (Act One) to *'La donna è mobile'* (Act Three). But here, in his *Scena ed aria* at the beginning of Act Two, the character is somewhat deepened. This is primarily through the expressiveness of his *cantabile, 'Parmi veder le lagrime'* ('Somewhere I see you crying') [18], in which the rhythmically free and expansive melodic line takes us some distance from the jauntiness of his Acts One and Three personae. Those who mechanically refer to the 'crudity' of Verdi's orchestration in *Rigoletto* should note the oboe's sustained A flat which adds a subtle new sonority to the section beginning *'Nei ei potea'*. The opera is full of such moments of refined orchestral thought. But the mood is brutally interrupted by the appearance of the courtiers, whose bouncy, syncopated narrative [19] brings us firmly back to the musical atmosphere of the opera's opening scene. The Duke's *cabaletta*, *'Possente amor mi chiama'* ('The power of love is calling'), is often cut in performance, but while its crude orchestration and heavy-footed melody do deflate the scene, this is at least better than the musical and dramatic non-sequitur which results if it is omitted.

Enter Rigoletto for the second and greatest of his *ariosi*. Marullo's apparently involuntary comment at the beginning — *'Povero Rigoletto'* — frames our central reaction to the spectacle of a man moving through a shattering and humiliating sequence of emotions. First comes the enforced gaiety of *'La-rà, la-rà'* [20], a pathetic attempt to maintain his court-jester's façade. The Page's interruption and Rigoletto's realization of the true state of affairs is set in a more fluid passage, with his mounting fury emphasized by a relentlessly repetitive string figure. *'Cortigiani, vil razza dannata'* ('Heartless bastards, you liars, you cowards') [21] comes at the moment when we would

20

Otakar Kraus and Joan Sutherland at Covent Garden in 1957. (Royal Opera House Archives)

expect, if convention were to be obeyed, a fast *cabaletta* in the manner of the Duke's *'Possente amor'*. This is in three sections, each in a different key, and each defined by a change in Rigoletto's state of mind. As the angry declamation of the first section is suffocated by tears, the obsessive string sextuplets give way to a more broken line and the vocal part shades almost into natural speech rhythms. With *'Miei signori'* [22], the understatement of the orchestral accompaniment (solo cello with *arpeggios* and a cor anglais doubling the vocal line) allows the exposed, murderously high, baritone part to reach its moment of greatest lyrical intensity.

After Gilda's entrance, Rigoletto rises to newfound authority in dismissing the courtiers; but now the focus is on Gilda. Unlike the other principals, her character develops in the course of the tragedy — in this respect she is clearly a precursor of Violetta in *La traviata*. Compare her narration here, *'Tutte le feste al tempio'* ('I was in church on Sunday') [23] with *'Caro nome'*. The luminous two-flute sonority of the latter now changes to a solo oboe while, in the melody, expressive triplets replace lively, *staccato* rhythms. Perhaps most tellingly, the vocal line, which in *'Caro nome'* seemed to delight in its own agility, now uses ornamentation in a far more economical manner, with no sense of surface decoration. Rigoletto answers Gilda with a static, broken line,

Elizabeth Harwood and Peter Glossop in the 1963 Sadler's Wells production. (photo: Donald Southern)

which eventually flowers into *'Piangi, piangi fanciulla'* ('Weep now, weep now my daughter') [24] where Gilda's propensity towards *fioritura* is transformed yet further from its childlike, naive associations.

The final part of the act injects unusual dramatic momentum into a conventional mould. The 'closed form' is, as we might expect, a fast, emphatic duet between Rigoletto and his daughter, *'Sì, vendetta, tremenda vendetta'* ('Give me a chance, I'll surely get you') [25]; but the bridge passage, in which Monterone is led off to prison, brings back the father's curse motif. The *cabaletta*-style duet is, almost inevitably, less meticulous in retaining individuality of musical expression between the two characters. As Verdi commented discussing this piece: 'I find it ineffective to have two characters singing about their affairs, one on one side, the other on the other, especially in *quick movements*'. But, on another level, Gilda's forcefulness here does something to prepare us for her changed vocal character in Act Three. At this stage of his career, Verdi was only conventional when it served his own idiosyncratic view of what opera demanded.

\* \* \*

The brief orchestral prelude to the final act — a mere nine bars long — is couched in what we might call Verdi's 'antique' vein, with suggestions of counterpoint and carefully prepared suspensions. But, as an earlier version in the sketchbook underlines, the passage is primarily concerned with emphasizing a single pitch — the note E. Just as *'Povero Rigoletto'* introduced the great scene in Act Two, here a short verbal exchange offers a succinct summary of the ensuing action: *Rigoletto:* 'E l'ami?' *Gilda:* 'Sempre.' (*Rigoletto:* 'You love him?' *Gilda:* 'Always.')

The restrained dialogue of father and daughter is interrupted by one of the most famous tunes in all opera, the Duke's *'La donna è mobile'* ('Women abandon us') [26]. It seems that Verdi was perfectly aware of the potential popularity of this melody; and also that its tunefulness could conceivably undermine its dramatic effect. For this reason he tried to prevent it becoming well-known before the first performance, only giving his tenor a copy of the music at the dress rehearsal. According to one eye-witness account, his careful preparations were more than justified:

> During the first performance of *Rigoletto*, when the violins of the orchestra announced that most elegant of motifs in the [third] act, the attentive public foresaw something new, and the tenor Mirate, seated astride a chair in Sparafucile's tavern, energetically and impudently attacked the piece. Hardly had the first verse finished before there arose a great cry from every part of the theatre, and the tenor failed to find his cue to begin the second verse. Verdi must have realized that the melody had always existed; he wished to shock the imagination with the commonplace fact that he had rediscovered it for himself.

But in actual fact the *Rigoletto* sketchbook gives us an earlier version of *'La donna'*, much simpler and more predictable:

Far from having 'rediscovered' the melody, Verdi obviously spent some time in honing it to his precise needs: a musical illustration of Byron's dictum that

*The set for Act Three of La Scala's 1961 production. (Teatro alla Scala)*

'Easy reading makes damned hard writing'.

If *'La donna'* is the best-known melody in *Rigoletto*, the Quartet which follows is the finest from a musico-dramatic point of view. Its opening section is sustained by a continuous orchestral argument (like the first two numbers of the opera). The characters converse freely over a rhythmically complex violin melody, and the delicacy of the orchestration, with *pizzicato* bass, and first violins moving freely above and below the vocal line, is well worth attention. The main movement, *'Bella figlia dell'amore'* ('If you want a faithful lover') [28, 29], although conventional in that it begins with a long tenor solo, is original in the way it retains the musical identity of the four soloists. The slight exaggeration of the Duke's ardent love-song sets a perfect perspective for the other three characters: Maddalena's wayward, chattering line; Gilda, at times with short, breathless phrases, at times rising lyrically above the others; Rigoletto, his insistence on vengeance keeping him firmly rooted to the bass line. It is a measure of Verdi's integrity that, even at the climax and coda, these musical personalities are maintained: in this sense, the Quartet is a perfect example of the new composer we find in *Rigoletto*.

The final numbers of the opera, the *Scena, Terzetto e Tempesta* and the last duet, are virtually unclassifiable in terms of conventional nineteenth-century opera. Although the former has a literally repeated trio at its centre, the surrounding mixture of static recitative, a storm which follows and punctuates the stage action, the reminiscences of the Quartet and *'La donna è mobile'*, gives the music a formal freedom quite unprecedented in this period and genre. There is throughout a superb economy of dramatic expression. In the opening recitative (*'Venti scudi hai tu detto'*) for example, Rigoletto's view of himself as an impersonal agent of justice (in answer to Sparafucile's request for the name of his victim the jester says, 'He is Transgression, I am Retribution') is matched by the austere restraint of the recitative, which Verdi specifically requests to be sung 'without the usual *appoggiaturas'*.

The music of the rising storm [30] is uncannily represented by, among other things, an off-stage male chorus humming chromatically; and the resulting atmosphere makes the Duke's sleepy reprise of *'La donna è mobile'* all the more jarringly effective. The trio itself, *'Se pria ch'abbia il mezzo'* ('I'll leave him alone till the first stroke of midnight'), has two contrasting ideas: the first

[31] in the minor, with driving rhythms, is in a sense completed by the second [32], which 'releases' Gilda from rhythmic constraint and allows her to articulate a pure, unornamented vocal phrase reminiscent of Violetta at the end of Act Two of *La traviata*. The close relationship of scenic and musical events becomes clear as the storm comes to a terrifying climax with the stabbing of Gilda (a thunder machine is requested in the score) before dying away to nothing.

In Verdi's battles with the censor over *Rigoletto* the sack which is delivered to the protagonist in the final scene came under criticism, presumably as a tasteless extravagance. Verdi's immediate defence of the device makes it plain that he considered it crucial to the timing of the closing moments. As he rightly pointed out:

> If you take out the sack it is unlikely that [Rigoletto] would talk to a corpse for half an hour before a flash of lightning reveals that it is the corpse of his daughter.

And because he, of course, wanted this revelation to occur *musically*, a more gradual chronological unfolding was necessary before the dramatic return of the Duke's *'La donna è mobile'*, again sharply jarring with the general musical background. The final duet with Gilda is a necessary point of stability within this frenetic closing sequence, and also presents an opportunity to recall obliquely past musical events. In the first part, *'V'ho ingannato'* ('It's all my fault'), Gilda's broken line is answered by Rigoletto in a phrase whose accompaniment perhaps carries an ironic reflection of Monterone's curse; in the second, *'Lassù in ciel'* ('Ah, soon in Heaven') [33], the solo flute *arpeggios* inevitably recall the innocent Gilda of *'Caro nome'*, and so remind us of how far this character has developed musically since that first aria. In the context, Rigoletto's final, anguished recollection of the curse itself is no more than a seal on the fact that the musical action has run its course.

\* \* \*

In the years immediately following *Rigoletto* Verdi made several comments on the opera. Most common are references to the unconventionality of Rigoletto as an operatic hero:

> Everyone cried out when I proposed to portray a hunchback on the stage. Well, I was quite happy to write *Rigoletto*. I found it extremely apt to depict this character, externally deformed and ridiculous, internally passionate and full of love.

At least one author has remarked that this aspect may have been somewhat overstressed, may not be at the heart of the work's originality. But such an attitude misses the basic point. Verdi was indeed fully aware of the opera's unusual dramatic structure:

> I conceived *Rigoletto* without arias, without finales, as an unbroken chain of duets, because I was convinced that that was most suitable. If someone remarks, 'But here you could have done this, there that' etc. etc., I reply: that might be excellent, but I was unable to do any better.

But, as we mentioned before, he was too acute a dramatist to conceive a work primarily in terms of formal considerations. The forms are unconventional because 'that was most suitable', because the particular nature of the characters determined the means by which they were musically articulated. And it is, of course, precisely this dramatic integrity which preserves *Rigoletto* as one of the cornerstones of the operatic repertory.

# The Timelessness of 'Rigoletto'

*Peter Nichols*

I suppose *Rigoletto* is the opera I have not seen more often than any other. I would never undervalue it. I am enthralled when I hear a reasonable performance of it which, because of its popularity, is not difficult to come by, and I certainly do not consciously avoid it. But, for someone living in Italy who is not Italian, there is perhaps a subconscious sense of avoiding it because it cuts very close to the bare bones of Italian problems. Painfully so: and, surely, this is a part of its constant success. I had the startling experience quite recently of taking off my earphones while listening to the opera only to hear the roar under the window, in real life, of a rather rough neighbour who shouted in broad Sicilian to his wife: 'I shall be back to kill you!'

The melodramatic threat across a sixteenth century square was a sharp reminder that Verdi, whose name was so closely tied to the patriotic movement for Italian unity, could also be the brilliant analyst of the defects of his people. This is the case with *Rigoletto*: it is a heroic condemnation of what can happen to a traditional form of Italian society, and it is as relevant today, in an Italy of the Mafia, or the Camorra, or even of the Red Brigades, as it was in the sixteenth century court of the Gonzagas of Mantua. Verdi settled for Mantua to meet the demands of the censor who wanted a reasonably remote background, and he was to see several other changes of background, from Scotland to Boston, in order to see his opera through the various censors of a still-divided Italy.

He knew from the beginning that he would have trouble with his subject. The play by Victor Hugo, *Le Roi s'amuse*, was produced on November 22, 1832 in Paris and lasted one performance, after which it was closed by the authorities. Hugo's play appeared at a time of political unrest. The opening followed a matter of days after an attempt on the life of Louis Philippe. It was not performed again for another fifty years when it failed again, this time with the public. Verdi saw great possibilities in the play as a basis for an opera. He must have sensed, however, that social unrest in the Italy of his time would make the censors extremely chary of a text which showed a ruler to be corrupt and licentiousness the norm. And, indeed, the Austrian censor in Venice, where the first production was due to take place, found it a scandalous text'of such repellent immorality and obscene triviality'. The one modern comparison with the opera is Berg's *Wozzeck* which also happens to have a baritone in the lead, humiliated by his superior who is also, like the Duke, a tenor, with the hero, in this case, demented rather than deformed but a similarly pathetic individual. Berg however showed his miserable Wozzeck as a symbol of all the under-privileged, and made his opera a hymn in favour of the unfortunate. But there is nothing of this saving altruism in *Rigoletto* and, in a sense, one can see why the censors saw the danger of this piece as a surgical study in the roots of violence and institutional instability just when institutions in the small states of the Italian peninsula were fragile. What the censors unwittingly did was to help Verdi show the timelessness of his creation.

Once *Rigoletto* was through the Austrian censors in Venice, its setting was changed twice (but otherwise with relatively minor mutilations) for two different productions in Naples where it appeared as *Clara di Perth* allegedly based on (sic) 'the novel of Scot', and then again as *Lionello*, while in Bologna

*Designs by Rosemary Vercoe for the 1982 ENO production by Jonathan Miller.*

and Rome it was given as *Viscardello*. This device of evading official displeasure by giving the work a setting free of immediate political or social relevance was common among Italian composers. Rossini's *Guillaume Tell* had, for instance, appeared in London as *Hofer, or The Tell of the Tyrol*, but in Milan as *Guglielmo Vallace*, in Rome as *Rodolfo di Sterlinga* and in Eastern Europe as *Charles the Bold*, because censors objected to the story of Swiss cantons rising in revolt against Austrian domination, and made more or less serious alterations to the text. But in the case of *Rigoletto*, the censors might be seen as giving a merited label of ubiquity to the opera: it made its points wherever it was set.

With, I would say, one limitation. It needs a claustrophobic atmosphere in which the Italian vices it portrays can emerge in a full vein of melodrama. The Mantuan court, as Verdi depicts it, is a sealed circle in which the venom of Rigoletto himself, the irresponsibility of power as personified in the Duke, the anarchic behaviour of the court and the work-a-day practice of professional assassination all have their effect without interference from outside or, even more to the point, from above. Verdi and Piave, his librettist, heighten this atmosphere by allowing just a few suggestions to penetrate this setting that somewhere, outside the vicious circle of the courtiers, there exists another world with principles.

Take for instance the minor character of Marullo. He is the courtier who first arrives with the sensational (and mistaken) news that Rigoletto has a mistress, and so can be seen as setting in motion the tragedy of Gilda's death. Yet, after her abduction, Rigoletto appeals directly to Marullo, pleading with him to say where the abductors have hidden Gilda:

Then I'll beg you, Marullo, I beg you.
You're a kind man at heart, you will help me.
Let me know where you've hidden her, my
    daughter?

Ebben piango, Marullo ... signore,
Tu ch'hai l'alma gentil come il core,
Dimmi tu dove l'hanno nascotto?

The suggestion is that Marullo still retains something of a human heart despite his presence at the Mantuan court. The appeal fails. In fact, Piave was rather too severe with his cuts here because in Hugo's play the Marullo-character is better explained: he is the court-poet to François I, Clément Marot, a commoner like the jester who might well have been expected to feel sympathy for another man of his own class. But even the hints left by Piave in this scene suggest that Rigoletto senses the existence of a world outside. So does Verdi's treatment of the Duke.

The Duke is more the central character of the opera than he is in Hugo's play, and almost certainly this is because he is a type only too familiar to Verdi and to successive generations of Italians. He is handsome, well-bred and powerful, as well as modern. The music Verdi gives him makes us hear that, from the cradle on, he has been told by his mother, by his sisters, by all the women he encounters and later by male sycophants, including Rigoletto, that as a well-endowed male, nothing can be denied him.

Verdi was right in giving his Duke a better part than Hugo gave his King François. The Duke survives in modern Italian life more than any of the other characters in the opera. This is quite obvious from a cursory look at the boutiques on Rome's Via Condotti or Monte Napoleone in Milan, where men's fashions serve personal vanity to a much greater and more varied extent than do women's fashions. Feminism has hit Italian women in terms of vanity and grace, but it has had little effect on the male view of himself. If anything, the Duke nowadays would be more prominent and typical than ever.

Two substantial changes were made in the part by Piave and Verdi. They cut out the scene in which the King produces the key to the room where the jester's daughter has locked herself and goes out, laughing, to rape her. Verdi authorised Piave to change words in his concessions to the censor but to keep all the situations intact, except this one. (He said that they could probably work out something better in any case.) And, secondly, they did not make him a member of the gang or kidnappers as Hugo did. This second change allowed Verdi to add a dimension to the Duke's character. He has little of the demonic energies of Don Giovanni, though Verdi knew Mozart's opera well, but the music he is given at the opening of the Second Act makes clear that he was genuinely in love with Gilda while she appeared to be out of his reach. As soon

*Designs by James Bailey for the 1947 Covent Garden production. (Royal Opera House Archives)*

as he is told that she has been kidnapped and brought to his own palace, and so is available to him, he breaks into *'Possente amor'*, which is without subtlety, and leads inevitably to the yet more self-satisfied *'La donna è mobile'*. That the Duke can delude himself into thinking he is in love suggests that he too is temporarily able to break out of the vicious circle around him. As a result he becomes more of a human being and less of a seduction machine.

Rigoletto himself provides another of these small chinks of light arriving from a better world when he tells Gilda about her mother, 'that angel' who felt pity for him and loved him despite his hump. Throughout the opera, he receives only mockery for his mis-shapen body, and he hates his deformity. Verdi will have known that there is no country where physical beauty is so valued as in Italy, and ugliness and deformity so despised. Women will still say: 'she is right to be jealous of him, he is a good-looking man'. They will never be heard saying that jealousy is in order because the man is good, or talented, or intelligent, or sensitive, or wise. Only if he is handsome need he be closely watched. And if, like the Duke, he has power as well, there is no holding him, because power which is not used is regarded like that miserably buried talent. His wife will seldom appear beside him, just as the Duke's wife is absent throughout the opera except for the portrait of her on the wall in the Second Act. The invisibility of wives survived as a social custom until quite recently – and still does in the more sheltered corners of Italian life.

Rigoletto, on the other hand, evokes the opposite emotion of repugnance because he is what nowadays it is fashionable to call 'handicapped' – and Italians are trying (but without conspicuous success) to feel for the *'handi cappati'*. In Rigoletto's mind the single reason for his failure to become a respected character at court, and to protect his own daughter, is the deformity which makes people, as a natural course, despise him. The lame and the mis-shapen are still regarded in traditional families as something shameful to keep hidden away and who, if let out, will only suffer yet more from the repugnance they will arouse.

| | |
|---|---|
| Heredity, human contact, | O uomini! O natura! |
| You made me evil, it was all your doing! . . . | Vil scellerato mi faceste voi! . . . |
| My destiny, always the hunchback! | O rabbia! . . . Esser difforme! . . . |
| My destiny, always the joker! | O rabbia! . . . Esser buffone! |

He explains that he hates himself because his deformity makes him despised while his master is young, gay, powerful and handsome. And so, to show his feelings towards the courtiers, he adopts a wounding tongue instead of a sword. It is an interesting comparison between two great national artists that Shakespeare, whom Verdi idolised, makes the hump-backed Richard III sexually attractive despite, or because of, his deformity while the crook-backed Italian is still incredulous that his 'angel' managed to love him. The courtiers for their part are incredulous that the monster can have a lover and choose the unpleasant method of kidnapping the supposed mistress in order to humiliate him, a type of crime common enough in modern Italy. They abduct his daughter while Monterone, the one voice from the world of conventional morality, curses him.

Yet, when he goes to the house where he keeps Gilda in secret, his change of mood does not really amount to the raising of the quality of his feelings, although he tries to make out to himself that it does. Verdi makes this passion for Gilda almost incestuous. And it is one based on fear of the violent atmosphere in which they live. He forbids her to set foot outside the house except to go to Mass (and the exception proves his rule that harm will come to her if she ventures out because it is at church that she encounters the Duke).

The first meeting on the stage between Rigoletto and Gilda is punctuated by his fears:

| | |
|---|---|
| Keep to your promise. | Ben te ne guarda! |
| As I came here did someone see me? . . . | Venendo mi vide alcuno? . . . |
| The door to the downstairs entrance . . . | . . . la porta che dà al bastione |
| You always lock it? . . . | È sempre chiusa? . . . |
| Oh, dear Giovanna, guard my daughter . . . | Ah! Veglia, o donna, questo fiore . . . |

He lives in a society which maintains its tension by this constant threat of violence. A knock on the door means trouble — *'Se talor picchian, Guardatevi d'aprire'* (literally: if someone knocks, be careful how you open . . . ) — and most of all if it is the Duke, despite the fact that theoretically he is the source of law and order as head of the state. He makes the laws and so, naturally, breaks the laws. Ironically — and Verdi underlines the irony — the one character scrupulously honest in his profession is Sparafucile, the paid assassin. He is perfectly aware that, at his level in the social structure, he can only give his clients confidence by nursing a reputation as a man of his word. And so he robustly refuses his sister's suggestion that he kill Rigoletto instead of the charming young man — the Duke though they are unaware of his identity — for whose murder Rigoletto has already paid Sparafucile half of the required sum in advance. The assassin behaves like a professional:

| | |
|---|---|
| Me murder the hunchback? . . . Is that what you're saying? | Uccider quel gobbo! Che diavol dicesti! |
| You think I'm a bandit? I'm some kind of robber? | Un ladro son forse? Son forse un bandito? |

*

The subject of violence is treated in three different ways. The most clearly defined level is that of the paid assassin who kills for profit. At a higher, and

*Lawrence Tibbett, the American baritone, as Rigoletto at the Met.*

*Carlo Cossuta as the Duke at Covent Garden. (photo: Donald Southern)*

*Robert Thomas, Anna Pollak, Frederick Sharp and Marjorie Shires in the 1955 Sadler's Wells production. (photo: Angus McBean © Harvard Theatre Collection)*

more anarchic, level there is the incipient violence in the life of the court. This violence can emerge as the result of a whim, or the prompting of the jester's twisted mind. When Rigoletto sees that his master wants to seduce the Countess of Ceprano, he proposes a series of fates for the tiresome husband: prison, exile or beheading. He may have little expectation that his suggestions will be adopted, but the effect of his constant pin-pricking is to heighten the atmosphere of menace at the court, already corrupt in other ways. The buffoon, in his attempts at irritating the courtiers, moreover displays the typical Italian confusion between malice and wit, or rather to suppose that malice is in fact wit. Even Verdi seems a little confused on the subject of humour in his opera. Although Rigoletto's outbursts are frequently said to be inspired by venom in his nature, the way in which Verdi deals with them, and with the exchanges between Rigoletto and Sparafucile, suggests that Rigoletto is adopting a wry form of black humour. There is a challenge here to the producer to raise some laughs even if the outstandingly Italian composer is rather muddled about his humourous intentions.

The third type of violence is that practised by Gilda. She is the only character in the opera allowed to mature. She passes from ingenuousness, due as much as anything to her seclusion, to great compassion by means of sexual experience. And in order to show this development, she has to go to the final recourse of stage-managing her own death. Some censors managed to impose a happy ending by arranging for Gilda to survive her stabbing. But that made a nonsense of the opera's fundamental meaning.

Mantua (or Perth, or Boston, or other settings imposed by the censors) remains as Verdi drew it a marvellous picture of a stagnant society, unchanging, but kept alive by the tensions imposed on it, mostly of a violent

*Luciano Pavarotti and Gillian Knight as the Duke and Maddalena at Covent Garden. (photo: Donald Southern)*

kind. Without violence, it would become fossilised, but it is not changed by violence. Rigoletto makes the fatal mistake of supposing that violence can be put to rational effect, to settle questions of right and wrong:

| | |
|---|---|
| He is Transgression, I am Retribution. | Egli e delitto, punizion son io. |
| (*Exit Rigoletto. It grows dark and thunders.*) | (*Parte: il cielo si oscura e tuona*) |

A modern terrorist would readily admit that violence cannot be used so precisely. Long accounts are extant of debates among terrorists as to whether killing or freeing their victims would have the greater effect. Even without the thunder to prompt him, Rigoletto should have known that violence is an imprecise weapon. In the event, the weapon explodes in his hand.

The very completeness of the opera enhances this idea of a closed and brittle society which, unlike the Duke's view of women, is far from *'mobile'*. It effectively resists change. No other opera of Verdi leaves one with the feeling that there is nothing more to be known about the characters and the background than what he has told us: in those final, almost peremptory notes, Verdi seems to be rubbing his hands with the greatest satisfaction at the thoroughness with which he has told his story — and at the brilliance with which he shows how traditional social habits can so easily make society degenerate into a closed, vicious and potentially violent pattern.

There are no other Europeans who, more than the Italians, take their time-honoured customs with them, and so Mantua could as well be exchanged as a background for the immigrant groups in the suburbs and shanty-towns of the big cities, or emigrant communities abroad. Some of the rules can be complicated, as Verdi showed. Dishonouring other people's daughters may be

31

*Derek Hammond Stroud and Valerie Masterson in Michael Geliot's production for ENO in 1976. (photo: John Garner)*

natural but, whoever you may be, you must not let it happen to your own daughter, or let her go unavenged. Even so, it is power that counts in the end, a dictum which most Italians would accept today. Rigoletto enjoys the feeling of triumph for a brief moment when he lets out his exultant cry over what he thinks is the dead body of the Duke ready in a sack to be thrown in the river:

> Ei sta sotto i miei piedi . . . E desso! Oh gioia!
> (*literally*: There he is at my feet . . . It is he! Oh joy!)

Wrong again. It is Gilda in the sack where, had they only realised it, the Duke had kept them all from the beginning. And surely the cold acuteness of the patriot Verdi's study of the defects of Italians, in these closed societies they build around themselves, explains a part of the unqualified and lasting popular success of an opera based on a play that failed.

# Thematic Guide

Many of the themes from the opera have been identified in the articles by numbers in square brackets, which refer to the themes set out on these pages. The themes are also identified by the numbers in brackets at the corresponding points in the libretto, so that the words can be related to the musical themes.

[7] **CHORUS** / *No. 5*

Vivace *sotto voce assai*

You dare to break in on to-day's ce - le - bra-
Oh tu che la fe - sta au - da - ce hai tur - ba-

tion, a mon -ster from Hell with a voice of dam - na -tion
to, da un ge - nio d'in - fer - no qui fo - sti gui - da - to;

[8] **RIGOLETTO**

Andante sostenuto

*p*

The old man laid his curse on me!
Quel vec - chio ma - le - di - va mi.

[9]

Andante mosso

*p*

[10]

Allegro vivo

*f*

[11] **RIGOLETTO**

Andante *con espressione*

*p*

Do not de - mand of one so sad
Deh non par - la - re al mi - se - ro

[12] **GILDA**

Andante *con agitazione*

*p*

Oh, sor - row and pain, sor - row and pain ... How
Oh quan - to do - lor! quan - to do - lor! che ____

hard to tell such bit - ter loss of love.
spre - me - re ____ si a - ma - ro ___ pian - to può!

34

[13] **RIGOLETTO**

Allegro moderato assai *affettuoso*

Oh, dear Gio - van - na, guard my daugh - ter,
Ah! ve - glia, o don - na, que - sto fio - re

she is ten - der as a flow - er
che a te pu - ro con - fi - da - i;

[14] **DUKE** / *No. 8 Duet*

Andantino *cantabile*

Love is the source of life, love is our sun - light.
E il sol dell' a - ni - ma, la vi - ta e a - mo - re;

[15] **DUKE** / *No. 8 Duet*

Vivacissimo

Fare- well, fare- well, my hope and hap - pi - ness.
Ad - di - o, ad - di - o spe - ran - za ed a - ni - ma.

[16] **GILDA** / *No. 9 Aria*

Allegro moderato *dolcissimo*

Dear - est name of my first love I'll re -
Ca - ro no - me che il mio cor fe - sti

mem - ber till I die.
pri - mo pal - pi - tar,

[17] **CHORUS** / *No. 10 Finale*

Allegro *sotto voce*

Soft - ly, soft - ly we move in to get her.
Zit - ti, zit - ti mo - via - mo a ven - det - ta,

[18] **DUKE** / *No. 11 Aria*

Adagio

*p cantabile*

Some - where I see you cry - ing
Par - mi ve - der le la - gri - me

[19] **CHORUS**

Allegro assai moderato

*p*

We went to look for her last night to - geth - er
Scor - ren - do u - ni - ti re - mo - ta vi - a

[20] **RIGOLETTO**

Allegro assai moderato

La rà, la rà, la la, la rà, la rà, la rà, la rà,

[21] **RIGOLETTO** / *No. 12 Aria*

Andante mosso agitato

*f* Heart - less bas - tards, you li - ars, you cow - ards,
Cor - ti - gia - ni, vil raz - za dan - na - ta!

[22] **RIGOLETTO**

Andante cantabile

*p* Oh my friends I am sor - ry, for - give me.
Miei si - gno - ri per - do - no, pie - ta - te

[23] **GILDA** / *No. 14 Aria*

Andantino

*p* I was in church on Sun - day as is my sa - cred du - ty.
Tut - te le fe - ste al tem - pio men - tre pre - ga - va Id - di - o,

[24] **RIGOLETTO**

Cantabile

*mf* Weep now, weep now my daugh - ter, my daugh - ter weep now.
Pian - gi, pian - gi, fan - ciul - la, fan - ciul - la, pian - gi.

[25] **RIGOLETTO**

Allegro vivo

*f* Give me a chance, I'll sure - ly get you.
Si, ven - det - ta, tre - men - da ven - det - ta.

[26] **DUKE** / *Canzone*

Allegretto con brio

*mp* Wo - men a - ban - don us, why should it hurt them
La don - na è mo - bi - le qual piu - ma al ven - to,

[27] **DUKE** / *No. 16 Quartet*

Allegro

*mf* When first I came to talk to you, I thought you ve - ry love - ly.
Un di, se ben ram - men - to - mi, o bel - la, t'in - con - tra - i,

**[28] DUKE**

Andante

If you want a faith-ful lov - er,
Bel - la fi - glia dell' a - mo - re,

**[29] MADDALENA**

Andante

You're a ly-ing sort of lov-er, all these com-pli-ments
Ah! ah! ri - do ben di co - re, chè tai be - je co - stan

**GILDA**

are easy Oh, I thought you were my lov - er,
po - co. Ah! co - si par - lar d'a - mo - re!

**[30] CHORUS** (*off-stage*)

Allegro

*(Humming)*

**[31] SPARAFUCILE**

Allegro

*f* I'll leave him a - lone till the first stroke of mid - night.
Se pria ch'ab-bia il mez - zo la not - te toc - ca - to

If any - one else comes I'll kill him in - stead.
al - cu - no qui giun - ga, per es - so mor - rà.

**[32] GILDA**

Allegro

*f* Fa - ther for - give me, give my your par - don,
Oh cie - lo pie - tà!

**[33] GILDA**

Andante

*pp* Ah, soon in heav'n when I'm near to my mo - ther
Las - sù, in cie - lo, vi - ci - na al - la ma - dre,

37

*Ettore Bastianini as Rigoletto (Teatro alla Scala)*

# Rigoletto

An Opera in Three Acts by Giuseppe Verdi
Libretto by Francesco Maria Piave
after Victor Hugo's drama 'Le Roi s'amuse'
English Translation by James Fenton

*Rigoletto* was first performed at the Teatro La Fenice, Venice on March 11, 1851. The first performance in England was at Covent Garden on May 14, 1853, and in New York on February 19, 1855.

This translation was made for Jonathan Miller's 1982 ENO production. It was felt that the setting of the opera could be successfully updated from an indeterminate Renaissance period in Mantua to the Cosa Nostra world of the New York Mafia in the 1950's. Stage directions matching this interpretation have been inserted at appropriate points, with footnotes giving the original directions in literal translations.

## THE CHARACTERS

The character descriptions in brackets reflect the 1982 ENO production.

| | |
|---|---|
| The Duke of Mantua (*The 'Duke'*) | *tenor* |
| Rigoletto *his Court Jester (a barman)* | *baritone* |
| Sparafucile a professional assassin | bass |
| Count Monterone *('Count' Monterone)* | *baritone* |
| Marullo | *baritone* |
| Borsa *Courtiers (members of the the Mafia 'family')* | *tenor* |
| Count Ceprano | *bass* |
| A Court Usher *(a henchman)* | *bass* |
| Gilda *Rigoletto's daughter* | *soprano* |
| Giovanna *her Duenna (Rigoletto's housekeeper)* | *mezzo-soprano* |
| Maddalena *Sparafucile's sister* | *contralto* |
| Countess Ceprano *(Ceprano's wife)* | *mezzo-soprano* |
| A Page *(a secretary)* | *mezzo-soprano* |
| Knights, Courtiers, Halberdiers (Members of the 'Family', Henchmen) | *tenors, basses* |

*The action, according to Piave and Verdi, takes place in Mantua, in the sixteenth century. This translation sets the action in Little Italy, New York, in the 1950s.*

*The set design model for Act One, scene two, by Patrick Robertson for the 1982 ENO production by Jonathan Miller.*

40

# Act One

*A hotel in New York under the control of the Mafia. A San Gennaro party is in progress. 'Ladies' and 'Gentlemen', and waiters.\* / No. 1 Prelude and Introduction. [8; 1, 2, 3, 4]*

**Scene One.** *Enter the Duke and Borsa.†*

### DUKE

That pretty girl I've been seeing in the city,
What say we bring the matter to a climax?

Della mia bella incognita borghese
Toccare il fin dell'avventura io voglio.

### BORSA

That little thing you've hung around at mass for?

Di quella giovin che vedete al tempio?

### DUKE

Seen her praying every Sunday.

Da tre mesi ogni festa.

### BORSA

Where does she live?

La sua dimora?

### DUKE

She's hidden in some sidestreet.
This strange man goes in there every evening.

In un remoto calle;
Misterioso un uom v'entra ogni notte.

### BORSA

Has she no notion
Who her lover is yet?

E sà colei chi sia
L'amante suo?

### DUKE

No notion.

Lo ignora.

*(A group of 'Ladies' and 'Gentlemen' cross the stage.)*

### BORSA

Come take a look! Some beauty.

Quante beltà!... Mirate.

### DUKE

Lucky Ceprano, his woman's really charming.

Le vince tutte di Ceprano la sposa.

### BORSA
*(quietly)*

He's coming. Keep your voice down.

Non v'oda il Conte, o Duca...

### DUKE

So what's the problem?

A me che importa?

### BORSA

He could mention to someone...

Dirlo ad altra ei potria...

### DUKE

Let him say what he wants. I'm not too worried.

Nè sventura per me, certo saria.

---

\* *A ballroom in the Ducal Palace. Upstage, a door leads onto other rooms equally splendidly illuminated. Ladies and Gentlemen, magnificently dressed; pages cross the stage. The celebration is at its height. Music can be heard at a distance and bursts of laughter from time to time.*
† *from a door upstage.*

## No. 2 Ballata in the Introduction [5]

Every woman is equally lovely.
I could fall for whatever's around me.
And I won't let one lover confound me.
When I'm loving there's no guarantee.
If her beauty's the cause of discovery
  It's her fate makes a woman disarming,
  Though today she seems utterly
    charming,
  Still tomorrow perhaps we will see.
Obligations and vows of devotion,
  I detest them like cruel diseases.
  Let the faithful keep faith if he pleases.
There's no point in love if a man is not
    free.
For the husband, the slave of emotion,
  For the furious lover – who needs him?
  Did some monster out of Hell have to
    breed him?
He holds no terrors, no worries for me.

Questa o quella per me pari sono
A quant'altre d'intorno mi vedo,
Del mio core l'impero non cedo
Meglio ad una che ad altra beltà.
La costoro avvenenza è qual dono
Di che il fato ne infiora la vita;
S'oggi questa mi torna gradita,

Forse un'altra doman lo sarà.
La costanza tiranna del core
Detestiamo qual morbo crudele,
Sol chi vuole si serbi fedele:
Non v'ha amor se non v'è libertà.

De'mariti il geloso furore,
Degli amanti le smanie derido,
Anco d'Argo i cent' occhi disfido

Se mi punge, una qualche beltà.

**Scene Two.** *Enter Ceprano, watching his wife, who is followed by a henchman, at a distance.*
*'Ladies' and 'Gentlemen' enter from all sides. At the back there is dancing\*. / No. 3 Minuet*
*and Perigordino in the Introduction.*

### DUKE
*(approaching Ceprano's wife and speaking to her, with much gallantry)*

You're going? That's cruel.

Partite? . . . Crudele!

### COUNTESS

My husband is leaving.
I have to go with him.

Seguire lo sposo
M'è forza a Ceprano.

### DUKE

Oh stay a little longer.
Your place is among us, the star of the
  party.
For you every heart here will long for
  possession.
For you make men love you, you set all
  hearts yearning,
  Destructive, alluring, a passion that's
    burning.

Ma dee luminoso
In corte tal astro qual sole brillare.

Per voi qui ciascuno dovrà palpitare.

Per voi già possente, la fiamma d'amore,

Inebria, conquide, distrugge il mio core.

*(He kisses her hand.)*

### COUNTESS

Don't speak like that . . .

Calmatevi . . .

**Scene Three.** *Enter Rigoletto, who meets Ceprano and the crowd.*

### RIGOLETTO

What's this that I see
On your forehead, Ceprano?

In testa che avete,
Signor di Ceprano?

*(The 'Count' makes an impatient gesture and follows the 'Duke'.)*

*(to the crowd)*

He's angry. You saw that?

Ei sbuffa! Vedete?

### CHORUS

What a party!

Che festa!

### BORSA

He's after the wife of Ceprano.

Il Duca qui pur si diverte! . . .

---

\* *The Minuet.*

42

Oh yes!
It's always like this here. There's nothing uncommon.
  The gambling, the drinking, the parties, the dances,
  The shooting, the eating, it's all fine for him.
And now there's a lady, he makes his advances.
The husband goes off with his head in a spin.

Oh sì!
Così non è sempre? che nuove scoperte!
  Il giuoco ed il vino, le feste, la danza,
  Battaglia, conviti, ben tutto gli sta.
Or della Contessa, l'assedio egli avanza,
E intanto il marito fremendo ne va.

(*Exit.**)

**Scene Four.** *Enter Marullo, in excitement. / No. 4 Chorus in the Introduction.*

MARULLO

Sensation! Sensation!

Gran nuova! gran nuova!

CHORUS

Marullo, what's happened?

Che avvenne? parlate!

MARULLO

You'll never believe it . . .

Stupir ne dovrete . . .

CHORUS

Come on then, impress us!

Narrate, narrate . . .

MARULLO

Our friend with the shoulder . . .

Ah! ah! . . . Rigoletto . . .

CHORUS

The fool?

Ebben?

MARULLO

It's revolting! . . .

Caso enorme! . . .

CHORUS

A new operation? . . . They've made him look normal? . . .

Perduto ha la gobba? Non è più difforme?

MARULLO

It's stranger than fiction! . . . The hunchback is hiding . . .

Più strana è la cosa! . . . Il pazzo possiede . . .

CHORUS

Is hiding?

Infine?

MARULLO

A lover . . .

Un'amante . . .

CHORUS

A lover? You're lying!

Un'amante! Chi il crede?

MARULLO

From hunchback to Cupid in three easy lessons! . . .

Il gobbo in Cupido or s'è trasformato! . . .

CHORUS

The hunchback a cupid? . . . There's hope for all then! . . .

Quel mostro Cupido! . . . Cupido beato! . . .

---

* Meanwhile the Perigordino is being danced at the back.

**Scene Five.** *Enter the Duke, followed by Rigoletto, afterwards Ceprano.*

**DUKE**
*(to Rigoletto)*

Ceprano's a nuisance. He won't let us be.     Ah più di Ceprano, importuno non v'è.
His lovely young woman's an angel for me!     La cara sua sposo è un angiol per me!

**RIGOLETTO**

Get off with her.                         Rapitela.

**DUKE**

You've said it. But how to?              È detto; ma il farlo?

**RIGOLETTO**

This evening.                        Stassera.

**DUKE**

And what of her husband?          Non pensi tu al Conte?

**RIGOLETTO**

Preventive detention.             Non c'è la prigione?

**DUKE**

Not that.                       No, no.

**RIGOLETTO**

Well then . . . retirement.         Ebben . . . s'esilia.

**DUKE**

Come on now, you're joking.       Nemmeno, buffone.

**RIGOLETTO**
*(gesturing to suggest decapitation)*

Alright . . . so then he goes missing.    Allora la testa . . .

**CEPRANO**
*(to himself)*

(He means what he's saying.)       (Oh l'anima nera!)

**DUKE**
*(tapping the 'Count' on the shoulder)*

Our friend here goes missing?       Che di' questa testa?

**RIGOLETTO**

An easy solution. Is he so important? But    E ben naturale! Che far di tal testa? . . . A
what use is he living?                 cosa ella vale?

**CEPRANO**
*(reaching for his knife\*, in a fury)*

You bastard!                       Marrano.

**DUKE**
*(to the 'Count')*

Lay off him!                    Fermate.

**RIGOLETTO**

I spit in his face!               Da rider mi fa.

**BORSA, MARULLO AND COURTIERS**
*(to themselves)*

He's angry and dangerous!        In furia è montato!

---

\* *unsheathing his sword.*

(*to Rigoletto*)

| You idiot, come here. | Buffone, vien qua. |
| Why can't you help pushing a joke to the [6] limit? | Ah sempre to spingi lo scherzo all' estremo. |
| The anger you challenge could hurt you like hell. | Quell'ira che sfidi colpir ti potrà. |

RIGOLETTO

| I have your protection. People don't scare me. | Che coglier mi puote? Di loro non temo; |
| I have your protection and no one dare touch me. | Del Duca un protetto nessun toccherà. |

CEPRANO
(*to the 'Family', aside*)

| Revenge on the madman. | Vendetta del pazzo ... |
| We all have a reason | Contr'esso un rancore |
| For hating the fool. | Di noi chi non ha? |
| Vendetta. | Vendetta. |

CHORUS

| But how to? | Ma come? |

CEPRANO

| Tomorrow at my place. | In armi chi ha core |
| You'd better come armed. | Doman sia da me |
| At nightfall. | A notte. |

ALL

| Alright. | Sarà. |

CEPRANO

| Revenge upon the madman ... | Vendetta del pazzo ... |
| We all have every reason | Contresso un rancore |
| For hating him for what he's done to put our lives in danger. | Pei tristi suoi modi, di noi chi non ha? |

(*The dancers fill the stage.*)

ALL

| Let's have music, let's have women, | Tutto è gioia, tutto è festa, |
| Let's have dancing through the day! | Tutto invitaci a goder! |
| Keep the couples always turning, | Oh guardate, non par questa |
| Dance and dance our lives away! | Or la reggia del piacer! |

**Scene Six.** *The same with Monterone. / No. 5 Continuation and Stretta of the Introduction.*

MONTERONE
(*off-stage*)

| I insist he sees me. | Ch'io gli parli. |

DUKE

| No. | No. |

MONTERONE
(*entering*)

| How dare you! | Il voglio. |

ALL

| Monterone! | Monterone! |

MONTERONE
(*proudly addressing the Duke*)

| Yes, Monteron ... My voice is like the thunder | Si, Monteron ... la voce mia qual tuono |
| Shaking your heart's foundations. | Vi scuoterà dovunque ... |

**RIGOLETTO**
*(to the Duke, mimicking Monterone's voice)*

I insist I see him.

Ch'io gli parli.

*(walking up to Monterone with mock gravity)*

You were discovered in your plot against me.

Voi congiuraste contro noi, signore,

But I took pity and forgave your treachery.

E noi, clementi in vero, perdonammo...

Are you out of your mind now . . . to come and blabber

Qual vi piglia or delirio . . . a tutte l'ore

About your daughter and her beloved honour?

Di vostra figlia a reclamar l'onore?

**MONTERONE**
*(looking at Rigoletto contemptuously)*

Another insult!

Novello insulto!...

*(to the Duke)*

I'll always be here to plague your banquets.

Ah sì, a turbare, ah sì, a turbare,

I'll come and shout here, I will torment you

Sarò vostr'orgie . . . verrò a gridare,

Until I'm given a proper vengeance

Fano a che vegga restarsi inulto

And satisfaction of our lost honour.

Di mia famiglia l'atroce insulto;

And if you torture me as well you may do

E se al carnefice pur mì darete,

You'll see me come again to haunt your table.

Spettro terribile mi rivedrete,

You'll see me come again until I'm given A proper vengeance from the world and Heaven.

Portante in mano il teschio mio, Vendetta chiedere al mondo e a Dio.

**DUKE**

Enough. Take hold of him.

Non più, arrestatelo.

**RIGOLETTO**

A madman!

È matto!

**BORSA, MARULLO, CEPRANO**

He's finished!

Quai delti!

**MONTERONE**
*(to the Duke and Rigoletto)*

You and your jester, I lay my curse on you.

Ah siate entrambi voi maledetti.

You set your jackal on the dying lion.

Slanciare il cane al leon morente

How I despise you . . .

È vile, o Duca . . .

*(to Rigoletto)*

and you, you serpent.

e tu serpente,

You who can laugh at this father's sorrow, See how I curse you!

Tu che d'un padre ridi al dolore, Sii maledetto!

**RIGOLETTO**
*(aside)*

(He cursed me. He cursed me.)

(Che sento? orrore!)

**ALL EXCEPT RIGOLETTO**

You dare to break in on today's celebration, [7] A monster from Hell with a voice of damnation.

Oh tu che la festa audace hai turbato, Da un genio d'inferno qui fosti guidato;

Your words are all vain, do not speak any longer.

È vano ogni detto, di quà t'allontana . . .

Go tremble old man, go in fear of our anger.

Va, trema, o vegliardo, dell'ira sovrana . . .

You dared to provoke us. Your hopes are all through.

Tu l'hai provocata, più speme non v'è.

Your curse will be fatal to no one but you.

Un'ora fatale fu questa per te.

*(Monterone is taken away by two henchmen; all the others follow the Duke into another room.)*

*(The curtain falls for a short time, so that the set may be changed.)*

46

**Scene Seven.** *A run-down street in the poorer section of Little Italy. The tenement, where Rigoletto lives, is on the left; next to it, in a disused open space where a building has been pulled down, is a net-ball court. Ceprano's place is on the opposite side of the street. Night. Enter Rigoletto, followed by Sparafucile. / No. 6 Duet.*

RIGOLETTO
(*to himself*)

(The old man laid his curse on me!)          [8] (Quel vecchio maledivami!)

SPARAFUCILE [9]

My friend ...                                      Signor? ...

RIGOLETTO

Look, I've got nothing.                             Va, non ho niente.

SPARAFUCILE

I'm not asking. You see before you          Nè il chiesi ... a voi presente
A man prepared to kill.                              Un uom di spada sta.

RIGOLETTO

A murderer?                                          Un ladro?

SPARAFUCILE

A man who'll help you                          Un uom che libera
Dispose of any rivals.                               Per poco da un rivale,
And you've a rival.                                  E voi ne avete ...

RIGOLETTO

Have I?                                              Quale?

SPARAFUCILE

You keep a woman in there.                     La vostra donna è là.

RIGOLETTO

(He knows me.) What would the charge be          (Che sento?) E quanto spendere
like
If it was someone important?                    Per un signor dovrei?

SPARAFUCILE

That would of course be extra ...           Prezzo maggior vorrei ...

RIGOLETTO

And how am I to pay?                            Com'usasi pagar?

SPARAFUCILE

Half in advance is usual,                      Una metà s'anticipa,
The balance when I've done ...                  Il resto si dà poi ...

RIGOLETTO

(The devil!) How do you manage              (Demonio!) E come puoi
Working outside the law?                            Tanto securo oprar?

SPARAFUCILE

Often I go in crowded streets,              Soglio in cittade uccidere,
Or even back at my place.                           Oppure nel mio tetto.
Wait for the man at nightfall ...                L'uomo di sera aspetto ...
One cut from this, he dies.                         Una stoccata, e muor.

---

* The end of a street that has no outlet. On the left, a house of neat appearance, with a courtyard, surrounded by a wall that has a door opening on the street. In the middle of the courtyard stands a large tall tree, and on one side a marble seat. At the top of the wall is a terrace, reached by a flight of steps in front of the courtyard, and leading into the rooms of the first floor. On the right, the high wall of the garden, and a wing of the palace of Count Ceprano. Night. Enter Rigoletto enveloped in his cloak, and followed by Sparafucile, carrying a long sword under his cloak.

(The devil!) And how, at your place?      (Demonio!) E come in casa?

**SPARAFUCILE**

Quite easily.                     È facile ...
My sister is my partner ...          M'aiuta mia sorella ...
She's a beauty, dancing and flirting.    Per le vie danza ... è bella ...
She knows what we're after ... and     Chi voglio attira ... e allor ...
   then ...

**RIGOLETTO**

I'm with you.                         Comprendo ...

**SPARAFUCILE**

No one notices.                   Senza strepito.

**RIGOLETTO**

I'm with you.                         Comprendo ...

**SPARAFUCILE**
(*showing his weapon*)

You see how sharp the blade is.      È questo il mio strumento.
You need it?                       Vi serve?

**RIGOLETTO**

Not for the moment.              No ... al momento ...

**SPARAFUCILE**

So much the worse.               Peggio per voi ...

**RIGOLETTO**

Who knows?                    Chi sa? ...

**SPARAFUCILE**

Sparafucil, remember me.         *Sparafucil* mi nomino ...

**RIGOLETTO**

A stranger?                   Straniero?

**SPARAFUCILE**
(*as he leaves*)

Not from these parts.             Borgognone.

**RIGOLETTO**

Just tell me, where should I find you?    E dove all'occasione? ...

**SPARAFUCILE**

Here every evening.              Qui sempre a sera.

**RIGOLETTO**

Go.                           Va.

**SPARAFUCILE**

Sparafucil, Sparafucil.         Sparafucil, Sparafucil.

**RIGOLETTO**

Go, go, go, go.               Va, va, va, va.

(*Exit Sparafucile.*)

**Scene Eight.** / *No. 7 Scene and Duet.*

**RIGOLETTO**
(*looking after Sparafucile*)

He's my equal. I have language, he has his    Pari siamo! ... io la lingua, egli ha il
   dagger,                               pugnale;
I am the man who mocks men, he has his    L'uomo son io che ride, ei quel che
   switchblade ...                         spegne! ...

The old man laid his curse on me! . . .
Heredity, human contact,
You made me evil, it was all your doing! . . .
My destiny, always the hunchback.
My destiny, always the joker.
Every day, every night, playing the fool
again.
Other men find relief in weeping. I cannot
weep.
Here comes my young employer,
Happy, attractive, influential, handsome.
In his cups he will tell me:
'Make us laugh, Rigoletto'.
I grit my teeth and do so . . . Condemned
to laughter!
How I hate you, you flattering group of
courtiers!
How I love it when I hurt you!
If my heart is cold, you are the ones who
changed me.
But in my home I can feel as a father.
The old man laid his curse on me. Oh that [8]
thought,
Why must it always return to haunt my
conscience? . . .
It is an evil omen? Oh no, this is madness.

Quel vecchio maledivami! . . .
O uomini! o natura!
Vil, scellerato mi faceste voi! . . .
O rabbia! . . . esser difforme! . . .
O rabbia! . . . esser buffone! . . .
Non dover, non poter altro che ridere! . . .
Il retaggio d'ogni uom m'è tolto . . . il
pianto! . . .
Questo padrone mio,
Giovin, giocondo, sì possente, bello,
Sonnecchiando mi dice:
Fa ch'io rida, buffone.
Forzar mi deggio, è farlo! . . . Oh,
dannazione!
Odio a voi, cortigiani schernitori! . . .

Quanta in mordervi ho gioia!
Se iniquo son, per cagion vostra è solo . . .

Ma in altr'uomo qui mi cangio! . . .
Quel vecchio maledivami! . . . Tal pensiero

Perchè conturba ognor la mente mia? . . .

Mi coglierà sventura? Ah no, è follia.

(*He unlocks the gate and enters the courtyard.*)

**Scene Nine.** *Enter Gilda.*

RIGOLETTO

Gilda!                                          Figlia . . .

GILDA

My father!                                 Mio padre!

RIGOLETTO

Here in your presence                 A te d'appresso
Always I find some cure for my sorrow.    Trova sol gioia il core oppresso.

GILDA

Oh, how I love you!                   Oh quanto amore!

RIGOLETTO

My one possession!                    Mia vita sei!
(*sighing*)
If you were gone from me what would I live    Senza te in terra qual bene avrei?
for?

GILDA

Oh, how I love you, dearest father.    Oh, quanto amore! Padre mio!
You seem distracted. What makes you    Voi sospirate! Che v'ange tanto?
worried?
Why can't you confide in your loving    Lo dite a questa povera figlia
daughter?
If there's a mystery, please just allow    Se v'ha mistero per lei sia franto
me . . .
Let me know something . . . who are my    Ch'ella conosca la sua famiglia.
family?

RIGOLETTO

No one but me.                        Tu non ne hai . . .

GILDA

Tell me your name then.              Qual nome avete?

Why should that matter?

A te che importa?

**GILDA**

Just tell me something,
Something about you . . .

Se non volete
Di voi parlarmi . . .

**RIGOLETTO**
(*interrupting her*)

Don't leave the house.

Non uscir mai.

**GILDA**

Only to mass.

Non vò che al tempio.

**RIGOLETTO**

Yes, that is well.

Or ben tu fai.

**GILDA**

If I've no sister, if I've no brother
Let me know this much – who was my
mother?

Se non di voi, almen chi sia
Fate ch'io sappia la madre mia.

**RIGOLETTO**

Ah, do not demand of one so sad
What was his former happiness.
She had an angel's pity,
A pity for my suffering.
I was a hunchback, penniless,
She gave me all her love.
Ah, she died. The earth is kind to her.
It covers her so gently.
You're all that's left to me . . .
(*sobbing*)
Oh God be thanked I have you!

[11] Deh! non parlare al misero
Del suo perduot bene,
Ella sentia, quell'angelo,
Pietà delle mie pene,
Solo, difforme, povero,
Per sompassion mi amò.
Moria . . . le zolle coprano
Lievi quel capo amato.
Sola or tu resti al misero,
Dio, sii ringraziato! . . .

**GILDA**

Oh, sorrow and pain . . . How hard to
tell
Such bitter loss of love.
Father, no more, don't speak of her . . .
You hurt me with such sorrow.
Why won't you let me know your name
And something of your sorrow?

[12] Oh quanto dolor! . . . che spremere
Si amaro pianto può?
Padre non più, calmatevi . . .
Mi lacera tal vista . . .
Il nome vostro ditemi,
Il duol che si v'attrista.

**RIGOLETTO**

What use to tell you? I have no name.
I am your father only.
Perhaps the world's afraid of me
And there are old resentments.
Others have laid a curse on me!

A che nomarmi? . . . è inutile!
Padre ti sono, e basti . . .
Me forse al mondo temono!
D'alcuno ho forse gli asti!
Altri mi maledicono!

**GILDA**

Tell me your homeland and where your
friends
And family are living.

Patria, parenti, amici

Voi dunque non avete?

**RIGOLETTO**

Homeland and family and friendship?
(*with passion*)
Homeland, my family, my universe is all
in you alone!
My Gilda dear, I worship you.

Patria! . . . parenti! . . . amici! . . .

Culto, famiglia, la patria,

Il mio universo è in te!

**GILDA**

If there was some way to make you more
happy!
That's all I want.

Ah, se può lieto rendervi,

Gioia è la vita a me!

The days are passing and I remain here.      Già de tre lune son qui venuta,
  I'm really longing to see the city.          Nè la cittade ho ancor veduta;
  If you allow it, perhaps I could . . .     Se il concedete, farlo or potrei . . .

RIGOLETTO

Not now! You promise you've never     Mai! . . . mai! uscita, dimmi, unque sei?
been outdoors?

GILDA

No.                          No.

RIGOLETTO

Sure?                    Guai!

GILDA

(Oh I'm lying.)               (Che dissi?)

RIGOLETTO

      Keep to your promise.             Ben te ne guarda!
(They could go after her, capture her  (Potrian seguirla, rapirla ancora!
  and rape her.
If they discovered she was a hunchback's  Qui d'un buffone si disonora
  daughter
How they would laugh and . . . oh no!)  La figlia, e se ne ride . . . Orror!)
(towards the building)
       Who's there?                     Olà?

**Scene Ten.** *Enter Giovanna.*

GIOVANNA

You called?                   Signor?

RIGOLETTO

  As I came here, did someone see me?     Venendo, mi vide alcuno?
  Come on, the truth now.           Bada, dì il vero . . .

GIOVANNA

    Ah no, how could they?             Ah, no, nessuno.

RIGOLETTO

Alright. The door to the downstairs     Sta ben . . . la porte che dà al bastione
  entrance . . .
  You always lock it?            È sempre chiusa?

GIOVANNA

    It's shut all day.               Ogner si sta.

RIGOLETTO

  Careful, the truth.             Bada, dì il ver?
Oh, dear Giovanna, guard my daughter.  [13] Ah! veglia, o donna questo fiore
  She is tender as a flower.         Che a te puro confidai;
  You are fond of her, you know her.   Veglia attenta, e non sia mai
  I entrust her to your care.        Che s'offuschi il suo candor.
From the wind that tears the blossom,  Tu dei venti dal furore,
  From the tempest in its anger,     Ch'altri fiori hanno piegato,
  Keep her safely from all danger.    Lo difendi, e immacolato
  Keep her innocent and fair.      Lo ridona al genitor.

GILDA

Such affection, such a sorrow!      Quanto affetto! . . . quali cure!
  Look to Heaven now, my father.    Che temete, padre mio?
  There's a God who watches over    Lassù in cielo, presso Dio
  And a guardian angel there.      Veglia un angiol protettor.
We are sheltered from misfortune.   Da noi stoglie le sventure
  We are hidden from all anger.     Di mia madre il priego santo!
  We're protected from all danger    Non fia mai divelto o infranto
  By my mother's holy prayer.     Questo a voi diletto fior.

51

**Scene Eleven.** *The Duke, disguised as a student, enters the street.*

RIGOLETTO

There's someone listening.                    Alcun v'è fuori . . .

*(Rigoletto opens the courtyard gate and, as he goes out to check the street, the Duke slips in and hides\*; he throws a purse to Giovanna to keep her quiet.)*

GILDA

Always,                              Cielo!

Always a new suspicion.                        Sempre novel sospetto . . .

RIGOLETTO
(turning to Gilda)

Last Sunday, was she followed home from      Alla chiesa vi seguiva mai nessuno?
mass?

GIOVANNA

No.                                            Mai.

DUKE

(Rigoletto!)                                   (Rigoletto!)

RIGOLETTO

Do not leave the latch off.                Se talor qui picchian,

Don't open to anyone . . .                     Guardatevi da aprire . . .

GIOVANNA

Even if they know you?                      Nemmeno al Duca? . . .

RIGOLETTO

Just do what I tell you. My daughter,          Non che ad altri a lui! . . . Mia figlia, addio.
goodbye.

DUKE

(His daughter!)                                (Sua figlia!)

GILDA

Goodbye, dear father.                      Addio, mio padre.

*(They embrace and Rigoletto, as he leaves, shuts the street gate behind him.)*

**Scene Twelve.** *Gilda, Giovanna and the Duke in the courtyard, afterwards Ceprano and Borsa in the street.* / *No. 8 Scene and Duet.*

GILDA

Giovanna, I should have told him.             Giovanna, ho dei rimorsi . . .

GIOVANNA

What do you mean?                           E perchè mai?

GILDA

Told him a young man followed us from          Tacqui che un giovin ne seguiva al
service.                                        tempio.

GIOVANNA

What good to tell him? Do you hate this        Perchè ciò dirgli? . . . l'odiate dunque
young man?
Do you want your father to stop him?           Cotesto giovin, voi?

GILDA

No. He is far too beautiful. He says he        No, no, chè troppo è bello e spira
loves me.                                       amore . . .

---

\* *behind a tree.*

And he seems such a kind man and very wealthy.

E magnanimo sembra e gran signore.

GILDA

I do not want his wealth. I've no ambition.
If he were penniless I think I'd love him
more in that condition.
Deep in my heart of hearts still dreaming
of him
I long to talk to him, tell him I love...

Signor nè principe... io lo vorrei:
Sento che povero... più l'amerei.
Sognando o vigile... sempre lo chiamo,
E l'alma in estasi... le dice t'a...

DUKE
(*appearing, signalling to Giovanna to leave them*)*

Love me!
Love me, repeat the words, oh how you
move me.
You'll open Heaven for me if you will
love me.

T'amo!
T'amo, ripetilo... si caro accento,
Un puro schiudimi... ciel di contento!

GILDA

Giovanna, Giovanna, oh where is she?

Is there no answer? Am I alone with
him?

Giovanna?... Ahi misera!!... non v'è
più alcuno
Che qui rispondami!... Oh! Dio...
nessuno!...

DUKE

You know me. I'll answer you with all
devotion.
When two are lovers what harm can
happen?

Son io coll'anima... che ti rispondo...
Ah due che s'amano... son tutto un
mondo!...

GILDA

Tell me what's happening. Who let you
in?

Chi mai, chi giungere... vi fece a me?

DUKE

Angel or devil, what's that to you?
I love you.

S'angelo o demone... che importa a te?
Io t'amo...

GILDA

Please leave me now.

Uscitene.

DUKE

You think I can leave you?
Now that I've heard you say how much
you love me?
No one can stop us now. Some kind of
destiny
Has bound your fate to mine for
evermore.
Love is the source of life, love is our [14]
sunlight.
His voice is heard when the heart is
beating.
Fame and prosperity, power, position,
They last a moment, their life is fleeting.
One thing's important, one thing worth
having,
The love the angels know, the Heaven of
loving.
If you will come to me, woman of
Heaven,

Uscire! adesso!...
Ora che accendene... un fuoco istesso!
Ah inseparabile... d'amore il dio
Stringeva, o vergine... tuo fato al mio!
È il sol dell'anima... la vita è amore,
Sua voce è il palpito... del nostro core...
E fama e gloria... potenza, e trono.
Umane, fragili... qui cose sono.
Una pur avvene... sola, divina,
È amor che agl'angeli... più ne avvicina!
Adunque amiamoci... donna celeste.

---

* *throwing himself at Gilda's feet.*

I shall be envied by all men on earth,
I shall be envied by all the world.

D'invidia agl'uomini ... sarò per te,
D'invidia agl'uomini ... sarò per te.

### GILDA

(In every fantasy, in every dream,
  The voice of tenderness, he speaks to
  me.)

(Ah de' miei vergini ... sogni son queste
  Le voci tenere ... sì care a me!)

### DUKE

Oh, tell me once more that you love me.

Che m'ami deh! ripetimi ...

### GILDA

You know it.

L'udiste.

### DUKE

I can't believe it!

Oh me felice!

### GILDA

I have one thing to ask you ...
Please tell me what your name is.

Il nome vostro ditemi ...
Saperlo non mi lice?

### CEPRANO
*(to Borsa, from the street)*

I think she's here.

Il loco è qui ...

### DUKE
*(thinking)*

I'll tell you then.

Mi nomino ...

### BORSA
*(to Ceprano, leaving)*

Alright.

Sta ben ...

### DUKE

Gualtier Maldè ...
A simple student, quite penniless.

Gualtier Maldè ...
Studente sono ... povero ...

### GIOVANNA
*(returning frightened)*

I think there's someone coming.

Rumor di passi è fuore ...

### GILDA

If it's my father ...

Forse mio padre ...

### DUKE

(If I could lay
My hands on the bastard
Who interrupts me.)

(Ah cogliere
Potessi il traditore
Che si mi sturba!)

### GILDA
*(to Giovanna)*

You take him down
And open the street door. Please go
  now.

Adducilo
Di quà al bastione, or ite ...

### DUKE

You'll always be mine.

Di': m'amerai tu?

### GILDA

And you?

E voi?

### DUKE

For ever after. Then ...

L'intera vita ... poi ...

### GILDA

No more, no more, please go now.

Non più ... non più ... partite ...

54

Farewell my hope and happiness.   [15]    Addio ... speranza ed anima
For you are mine for ever.               Sol tu sarai per me.
My love will never turn away         Addio ... vivrà immutabile
From you. I need you.                L'affeto mio per te. Addio.

(*Exit the Duke into the street with Giovanna. Gilda follows the Duke with her eyes.*)

**Scene Thirteen.** / *No. 9 Scene and Aria.*

GILDA

Gualtier Maldè, you were the first to love me      Gualtier Maldè! ... nome di lui si amato
And my heart will be true to you for ever.      Ti scolpisci nel core innamorato!

Dearest name of my first love   [16]   Caro nome che il mio cor
  I'll remember till I die             Festi primo palpitar,
  All the pleasure that you gave,      Le delizie dell'amor
  All the longings and the sighs,      Mi déi sempre rammentar!
  How my heart would beat so fast      Col pensier il mio desir
  With a passion like a flame,      A te sempre volerà,
And until, until the last            E fin l'ultimo sospir,
  I'll remember your dear name.      Caro nome, tuo sarà.

(*As she walks along the balcony and goes into the building, her voice gradually fades away.** *)

**Scene Fourteen.** *Marullo, Ceprano, Borsa, Henchmen, masked and armed. Gilda on the balcony.*

BORSA
(*to the Chorus, indicating Gilda*)
She's there.      È là.

CEPRANO
  Just look at her.      Miratela ...

CHORUS
  The purest beauty.      Oh quanto è bella!

MARULLO
Some sort of vision.      Par fata od angiol.

CHORUS
  The secret mistress of Rigoletto,      L'amante è quella
So sweet and gentle.      Di Rigoletto!

**Scene Fifteen.** *Enter Rigoletto, in thought.* / *No. 10 Scene and Finale I.*

RIGOLETTO
(Something draws me back. But why?)      (Riedo! ... perchè?)

BORSA
No talking. To business. Stay close to me.)      Silenzio ... all'opra ... badate a me.

RIGOLETTO
(How the old man cursed me ... he cursed [18] (Ah da quel vecchio fui maledetto!)
me.)

CEPRANO
What was that?      Chi va là?

BORSA
(*to his companions*)
  Be quiet. It's Rigoletto.      Tacete ... c'è Rigoletto.

---

* She carries a lantern.

**CEPRANO**

Let's kill the hunchback. Two birds in one.

Vittoria doppia! . . . l'uccideremo.

**BORSA**

Wait till tomorrow. We want our fun.

No, chè domani più rideremo . . .

**MARULLO**

Leave this to me now.

Or tutto aggiusto . . .

**RIGOLETTO**

(I know that voice.)

(Chi parla quà?)

**MARULLO**

Hey, Rigoletto.

Ehi Rigoletto? . . . Di?

**RIGOLETTO**
(*in a terrifying voice*)

(Say, who is that?)

(Chi va là?)

**MARULLO**

Don't bite my head off. It's . . .

Eh non mangiarmi! . . . Son . . .

**RIGOLETTO**

Who?

Chi?

**MARULLO**

Marullo.

Marullo.

**RIGOLETTO**

It's black as pitch here. I did not see you.

In tanto bujo lo sguardo è nullo.

**MARULLO**

We've got a job on. You feel like coming?
We're going after Ceprano's woman.

Qui ne condusse ridevol cosa . . .
Tôrre a Ceprano vogliam la sposa.

**RIGOLETTO**

(Thank God, Ceprano!) So what's the plan then?

(Ahimè respiro! . . . ) Ma come entrare?

**MARULLO**
(*to Ceprano*)

You've got your door key?

La vostra chiave?

(*to Rigoletto*)

No need to worry.
The plan is foolproof. It's working smoothly.

Non dubitare,
Non dee mancarci lo stratagemma . . .

(*He gives him the keys obtained from Ceprano.*)

Here is the door key.

Ecco la chiave . . .

**RIGOLETTO**
(*feeling the keys*)

I've seen it on him.

Sento il suo stemma.

(*breathing more freely*)

(So I was wrong then. They have not seen her.)
His place is that one. I'll come and help you.

(Ah terror vano fu dunque il mio!)
N'è là il palazzo . . . con voi son io.

**MARULLO**

Want one of these things?

Siam mascherati . . .

**RIGOLETTO**

I'd better have one.
Come on. Give it over.

Ch'io pur mi mascheri;
A me una larva?

## MARULLO

I've got one here.                   Sì, pronta è già.
You take the ladder.          Terrai la scala...

(*He puts a mask on Rigoletto's face, and at the same time binds it with a handkerchief; he leads him to hold steady a ladder which they have placed against the tenement balcony.*)

### RIGOLETTO

It's even darker now.          Fitta è la tenebra...

### MARULLO
(*to his companions*)

The mask will make him as blind as a     La benda cieco e sordo il fa.
bat.

### ALL

Softly, softly we move in to get her.  [17]  Zitti, zitti moviamo a vendetta,
Now's the moment for our vendetta.       Ne sia côlto or che meno l'aspetta.
He would mock us and put us in         Derisore si audace costante
   danger.
He would laugh at us. Now it's his       A sua volta schernito sarà!...
   turn.
Gently, gently we'll capture his mistress  Cheti, cheti, rubiamgli l'amante,
And tomorrow we'll laugh him to      E la corte doman riderà.
   scorn.
Be careful now and not a sound.        Zitti, cheti, attenti all'opra.

(*Some go up on to the balcony, break down the first floor door, then go down and open the street gate to the others, who enter and drag away Gilda, who is gagged with a handkerchief. Crossing the courtyard she loses a scarf.*)

### GILDA
(*from a distance*)

Oh help me, father, help me...     Soccorso, padre mio...

### CHORUS

We've got her!                 Vittoria!...

### GILDA
(*farther still*)

Oh help me!                   Aita!

### RIGOLETTO

How long must this go on for? What are  Non han finito ancor!...qual derisione...
   they doing?
              (*touching his eyes*)
What have they done to me?      Sono bendato!...

(*He snatches off the handkerchief and mask, and recognises the scarf,\* sees the open door, enters, and drags out a frightened Giovanna; he stares at her, and after many efforts to speak, he exclaims:*)

Ah! Now the curse is working!     Ah!...la maledizione!!†

*Curtain.*

---

\* *by the light of a forgotten lantern,*
† (*He faints.*)

# Act Two

**Scene One.** *As Act One.* * *Enter the Duke, much agitated. / No. 11 Prelude, Scene and Aria.*

DUKE

Somebody came and stole her,
But when? By God . . . All in a moment,
As I began to feel some danger.
I hurried back there to find out what had
  happened.
The door was open, the house was deserted.

And where can they have hidden my dear
  angel?
No other woman has ever had such power
To make me feel that I could love her for
  ever.
She was so innocent, so modest in manner,
I could almost have believed myself a new
  man.
Somebody came and stole her!
But who would dare to? Ah, I'll not hesitate
  to have my vengeance.
Oh, if she's weeping, she must have comfort.

Ella mi fu rapita!
E quando, o ciel? . . . ne' brevi istanti, prima
Che il mio presagio interno
Sull'orma corsa ancora mi spingesse!

Schiuso era l'uscio! . . . e la magion
  deserta! . . .
E dove ora sarà quell'angiol caro? . . .

Colei che prima potè in questo core
Destar la fiamma di costanti affetti? . . .

Colei si pura, al cui modesto sguardo
Quasi spinto a virtù talor mi credo! . . .

Ella mi fu rapita! . . .
E chi l'ardiva? . . . ma ne avrò vendetta:

Lo chiede il pianto della mia diletta.

Somewhere I see you crying
  And calling in desperation,
  Weeping in doubt and terror
  Beset by an unknown danger.
  Maybe my name occurs to you,
  You call on your Gualtier.

I could not find you anywhere,
  I could not rescue my lover,
  Though I'd have given anything,
  Anything for your safety.
  Nothing would have been too hard for
    me to bear
  To find my dearest love.

[18]  Parmi veder le lagrime,
  Scorrenti da quel ciglio,
  Quando fra il dubbio è l'ansia
  Del subito periglio
  Dell'amor nostro memore,
  Il suo Gualtier chiamò.

Ne dei potea soccorrerti,
  Cara fanciulla amata;
  Ei che vorria dell'anima,
  Farti quaggiù beata;
  Ei che le sfere agl'angeli

  Per te non invidiò.

**Scene Two.** *Enter Marullo, Ceprano, Borsa and other members of the 'Family'.*

ALL

Listen, listen!

Duca, Duca?

DUKE

What's that?

Ebben?

ALL

We've got the secret mistress
of Rigoletto!

L'amante
Fu rapita a Rigoletto.

---

* *A room in the Ducal Palace. Doors right and left, and one at the back. On one side of the door
hangs a full-length portrait of the Duke, on the other, one of the Duchess. An armchair stands
by a table covered in velvet cloth, and other furniture.*

| | |
|---|---|
| How? Where was she? | Come! e d'onde? |

ALL

| | |
|---|---|
| In a hide-out. | Dal suo tetto. |

DUKE

| | |
|---|---|
| Ha! ha! Tell me. What do you mean? | Ah, ah! dite come fu? |

ALL

| | |
|---|---|
| We went to look for her last night together [19] | Scorrendo uniti remota via |
| A little after the sun had set. | Brev'ora dopo caduto il dì: |
| We'd heard about her, about her beauty. | Come previsto ben s'era in pria, |
| We made a plan, and there we met. | Rara beltà ci si scoprì. |
| She was the lover of Rigoletto. | Era l'amante di Rigoletto |
| We saw her once and then she | Che, vista appena, si dileguò. |
| disappeared. | |
| And we were wondering just how to get her | Già di rapirla s'avea il progetto, |
| When all at once her man was there. | Quando il buffone vêr noi spuntò: |
| But when we told him that we were after | Che di Ceprano noi la contessa |
| Ceprano's woman, it made him grin, | Rapir volessimo, stolto, credè; |
| And so we got him to hold the ladder | La scala quindi all'uopo messa, |
| And wear a blindfold and help us in. | Bendato, ei stesso ferma tenè, |
| It took a minute then to get his lover | Salimmo, e rapidi la giovinetta |
| And take her off beneath his very nose. | A noi riusciva quindi apportar. |
| You can imagine, when he discovered, | Quand'ei s'accorse della vendetta |
| He cursed the world for all his woes. | Restò scornato ad imprecar. |

DUKE
(*to himself*)

| | |
|---|---|
| (Never. They've found her, my loved one.) | (Cielo! . . . è dessa la mia diletta! . . . ) |

(*aloud*)

| | |
|---|---|
| What have you done with her, where can I find her? | Ma dove or trovasi, la poveretta? . . . |

ALL

| | |
|---|---|
| We brought her here for you to see. | Fù da noi stessi addotta or qui. |

DUKE
(*to himself*)

| | |
|---|---|
| (So fortune still is good to me. | (Ah tutto il ciel non mi rapì! |
| The power of love is calling, | Possente amor mi chiama, |
| I cannot disobey it. | Volar io deggio a lei; |
| I'd give my wealth away | Il serto mio darei |
| To win my lover's hand. | Per consolar quel cor. |
| It may be she will have to know | Ah! sappia alfin chi l'ama |
| Exactly who I am now. | Conosca appien chi sono, |
| She'll have to know that all men | Apprenda ch'anco in trono |
| Are slaves to Love's commands.) | Ha degli schiavi Amor.) |

ALL
(*among themselves*)

| | |
|---|---|
| (You see the way his face has changed. | (Oh qual pensier or l'agita; |
| What can it mean? | Come cangiò d'umor! |
| There's something going on. | Oh qual pensier or l'agita, |
| What can it be?) | Come cangiò d'umor!) |

(*Exit Duke, quickly*)

**Scene Three.** *Marullo, Ceprano, Borsa and other members of 'the Family'; then Rigoletto enters, from the right, singing softly and trying to conceal his grief. / No. 12 Scene and Aria.*

MARULLO

| | |
|---|---|
| Poor little Rigoletto . . . | Povero Rigoletto! . . . |

RIGOLETTO
(*off-stage*)

| | |
|---|---|
| La rà, la rà, la là, la rà . . . | La rà, la rà, la là, la rà . . . |

## CHORUS

Be quiet, he's coming.                              Ei vien! . . . silenzio.
(*Rigoletto appears, pretending indifference.*)

### ALL

Oh good morning, Rigoletto.                     Oh buon giorno, Rigoletto.

### RIGOLETTO

(They're in it all together.)                       (Han tutti fatto il colpo!)

### CEPRANO

What's the latest                                          Ch'hai di nuovo,
With you?                              Buffon?

### RIGOLETTO
(*imitating him*)

What's the latest with you?                Ch'hai di nuovo, buffon?
That you are even more boring than usual.    Che dell'usato più noioso voi siete.

### ALL

Ha! Ha! Ha!                                                          Ah! Ah! Ah!

### RIGOLETTO
(*looking round uneasily*)

(Where would they keep her hidden?)    (Ove l'avran nascosta? . . . )

### ALL

(He's looking for his lover.)                   (Guardate com'è inquieto!)

### RIGOLETTO

I'm so happy                                          Son felice
You didn't catch pneumonia            Che nulla a voi nuocesse
Out late in such bad weather.          L'aria di questa notte . . .

### MARULLO

I was sleeping.                                                 Questa notte!

### RIGOLETTO

Oh, what a stroke of genius!              Si . . . Ah fu il bel colpo! . . .

### MARULLO

I'm such a heavy sleeper.                                S'ho dormito sempre!

### RIGOLETTO

Ah, you were sleeping. Well perhaps I just    Ah, voi dormiste! . . . avrò dunque sognato!
dreamt it.
(*He walks away and, seeing a scarf on the table, scrutinises it.*)

### ALL

(Look, look, searching for his lover.)    (Ve' come tutto osserva!)

### RIGOLETTO
(*throwing it away*)

(It's not Gilda's.)                                          (Non è il suo.)
Is the Duke still asleep?              Dorme il Duca tuttor?

### ALL

Yes, he is sleeping.                                    Si, dorme ancora.

**Scene Four.** *Enter a secretary.**

### SECRETARY

Where's the boss? I've a message from his    Al suo sposo parlar vuol la duchessa.
lawyer.

---

* page of the Duchess.

**CEPRANO**

| | |
|---|---|
| He's sleeping. | Dorme. |

**SECRETARY**

| | |
|---|---|
| Why, I thought I saw him with you. | Qui or or con voi non era? |

**BORSA**

| | |
|---|---|
| Well, he's busy. | È a caccia. |

**SECRETARY**

| | |
|---|---|
| I've a message. It's urgent. | Senza paggi! ... senz'armi! ... |

**ALL**

| | |
|---|---|
| He's left his orders. | E con capisci |
| He cannot be disturbed for any reason. | Che per ora vedere non può alcuno? ... |

**RIGOLETTO**
(*who has listened attentively, suddenly exclaims:*)

| | |
|---|---|
| Ah, she is with him then! She is upstairs! | Ah ella è qui dunque! ... Ella è col Duca! |

**ALL**

| | |
|---|---|
| Who? | Chi? |

**RIGOLETTO**

| | |
|---|---|
| The girl you stole last night | La giovin che stanotte |
| When you tricked me into helping. | Al mio tetto rapiste ... |
| But I will get her back now. She's up there. | Ma la saprò riprender ... Ella è là ... |

**ALL**

| | |
|---|---|
| If your mistress has vanished, go find | Se l'amante perdesti, la ricerca |
| Another. | Altrove. |

**RIGOLETTO**

| | |
|---|---|
| I want my daughter. | Io vo' mia figlia ... |

**ALL**

| | |
|---|---|
| She's his daughter! | La sua figlia! |

**RIGOLETTO**

| | |
|---|---|
| Yes, she is my daughter. Such a noble victory, | Sì, la mia figlia ... D'una tal vittoria ... |
| Eh? Why don't you laugh your hearts out? | Che? ... adesso non ridete? ... |
| She's back up there. Let me see her. Oh, give her back to me. | Ella è là ... la vogl'io ... la renderete. |

(*He runs towards the door, but henchmen prevent him leaving.*)

[21]

| | |
|---|---|
| Heartless bastards, you liars, you cowards. | Cortigiani, vil razza dannata, |
| How much money did my daughter bring you? | Per qual prezzo vendeste il mio bene! |
| Is there nothing too precious for money? | A voi nulla per l'oro sconviene, |
| She's my daughter, my great and only joy. | Ma mia figlia è impagabil tesor. |
| Let me see her. Though I know I've no weapon | La rendete ... o, se pur disarmata, |
| I will fight with my hands till I have her. | Questa man per voi fora cruenta; |
| There's no trace of a fear in a father | Nulla in terra più l'uomo paventa, |
| When defending his daughter's good name. | Se dei figli diffende l'onor. |
| Let me through now. Let me see her. I must see my daughter. | Quella porta, assassini, m'aprite. |

(*He goes again to the door, but he is prevented from opening it; after a struggle he returns centre-stage.*)

| | |
|---|---|
| Ah, I know it, all against me. Hated, every one. | Ah! voi tutti a me contro venite! |

(*weeping*)

| | |
|---|---|
| Then I'll beg you, Marullo, I beg you. | Ebben piango . . . Marullo . . . signore, |
| You're a kind man at heart, you will help me. | Tu ch'hai l'alma gentil come il core, |
| Let me know where you've hidden her, my daughter. | Dimmi tu, dove l'hanno nascosta? . . . |
| She's there. Will you tell me. You hate me. I know. | È là? . . . Non è vero? . . . tu taci! . . . ohime! . . . |
| Oh my friends, I am sorry, forgive me. [22] | Miei signori . . . perdono, pietate . . . |
| Let me go to my daughter and see her. | Al vegliardo la figlia ridate . . . |
| Is it so much to ask you to see her? | Ridonarla a voi nulla ora costa, |
| She is nothing to you now, | A voi nulla ora costa, |
| But she's all that I own. She's my only child. | Tutto al mondo è tal figlia per me. |
| Forgive me my friends, forgive me, | Signori, perdon, perdono, |
| Forgive me. Oh let me see my daughter, | Pietà, ridate a me la figlia; |
| She is everything, all that I have. | Tutto al mondo è tal figlia per me: |
| Have pity on my daughter. | Ridate a me la figlia, |
| She is the one thing I love. | Pietà, signori, pietà. |

**Scene Five.** *Enter Gilda, who throws herself into her father's arms. / Nos. 13 and 14 Scene, Chorus and Duet.*

### GILDA

| | |
|---|---|
| My father! | Mio padre! |

### RIGOLETTO

| | |
|---|---|
| Gilda, my Gilda! | Dio! mia Gilda! . . . |
| You see her, my daughter, | Signori, in essa è tutta |
| My Gilda is all I have now. But I see you're frightened. | La mia famiglia . . . Non temer più nulla, |
| My little angel . . . don't worry, they were teasing. | Angelo mio . . . fù scherzo, non è vero? |

(*to the crowd*)

| | |
|---|---|
| I was so worried. It's over. | Io che pur piansi or rido . . . |

(*to Gilda*)

| | |
|---|---|
| But why are you weeping? | E tu a che piangi? |

### GILDA

| | |
|---|---|
| Oh, father, I'm ashamed. | Ah! l'onta, padre mio! |

### RIGOLETTO

| | |
|---|---|
| Tell me, what's happened? | Ciel! che dici? |

### GILDA

| | |
|---|---|
| I cannot tell you in front of all these people. | Arrossir voglio innanzi a voi soltanto . . . |

### RIGOLETTO
(*to the assembled crowd, in a commanding manner*)

| | |
|---|---|
| Leave us alone together | Ite di quà, voi tutti . . . |
| And if the Duke himself should dare to approach us | Se il Duca vostro d'appressarsi osasse, |
| Tell him not to disturb us. That is my order. | Ch'ei non entri gli dite, e ch'io ci sono. |

(*He throws himself onto the chair.*)

### ALL
(*aside*)

| | |
|---|---|
| (Rigoletto's going crazy. | (Coi fanciulli a co' dementi |
| We'll pretend to play his game. | Spesso giova il simular. |
| We can watch him from the next room. | Partiam pur, ma quel ch'ei tenti |
| Let us leave him to his shame.) | Non lasciamo d'osservar.) |

(*Exeunt, shutting the door behind them.*)

62

## Scene Six. *Gilda and Rigoletto.*

**RIGOLETTO**

Speak now. They've left us.

Parla . . . siam soli.

**GILDA**

(God, give me the courage.)
I was in church on Sunday          [23]
  As is my sacred duty.
He turned around and gazed at me,
  He had a fatal beauty.
Silently as our eyes would meet
  Our hearts were joined in one.
Yesterday night he came to me,
  Spoke with a deep emotion:
'I am a student, penniless' –
  Told me his true devotion.
Wooed by his sighing and longing
  Our love has already begun.
He went his way. Now my heart was full
  of love.
I could not help believing him.
All of a sudden those men appeared
And forced me to go with them.
They tied me up and brought me here
  In terror for my life.

(Ciel, dammi coraggio!)
Tutte le feste al tempio
  Mentre pregava Iddio,
Bello e fatale un giovane
  Offriasi al guardo mio . . .
Se i labbri nostri tacquero,
  Dagl'occhi il cor parlò.
Furtivo fra le tenebre
  Sol ieri a me giungeva . . .
'Sono studente, povero,'
  Commosso mi diceva,
E con ardente palpito
  Amor mi protestò.
Partì . . . il mio core aprivasi

A speme più gradita,
Quando improvvisi apparvero
Color che m'han rapita,
E a forza qui m'addussero
Nell'ansia più crudel.

**RIGOLETTO**

Ah, I prayed to bear the shame alone.
  God give me all the sorrow.
Let her ascend to Heaven now.
  Let me alone be harrowed.
We need to pray to God above
  When we are near the gallows.
The future, everything's hollow.
  The altar is overthrown.
Ah, weep now, my daughter.          [24]
Burden my heart with your sorrow
  and pain.

Ah! Solo per me l'infamia
A te chiedeva, o Dio . . .
Ch'ella potesse ascendere
Quanto caduto er'io . . .
Ah! presso del patibolo
Disogna ben l'altare! . . .
Ma tutto ora scompare . . .
L'altar si rovesciò!
Piangi, fanciulla, e scorrer,
Fà il pianto sul mio cor.

**GILDA**

Father, you are my comfort.
Oh, please console my shame.

Padre, in voi parla un angel
Per me consolator.

**RIGOLETTO**

I've one thing to do here before I am
  finished;
As soon as it's over we'll go from the city.

Compiuto pur quanto a fare mi resta,

Lasciare potremo quest'aura funesta.

**GILDA**

Yes.

Si.

**RIGOLETTO**

(A day is enough to do all that I need.)

(E tutto un sol giorno cangiare potè!)

## Scene Seven. *Enter a henchman with Monterone, crossing the stage surrounded by other henchmen.*

**HENCHMAN**

Move back there. Monterone must go to
  his death.

Schiudete, ire al carcere Monteron dee.

**MONTERONE***

I see that my curse could not harm or
  destroy you.
Your life bears a charm which protects
  you from vengeance.

Poichè fosti invano da me maledetto,

Nè un fulmine o un ferro colpiva il tuo
  petto

---

* *(stopping by the portrait)*

63

| You'll always be happy and I shall have lost. | Felice pur anco, o Duca, vivrai . . . |

*(Exeunt.)*

**RIGOLETTO**

| Old man, you're mistaken. You'll have your revenge. | No, vecchio, t'inganni . . . un vindice avrai. |

**Scene Eight.** *Rigoletto and Gilda.*

**RIGOLETTO**

| Give me a chance I'll surely get you. [25] | Si, vendetta, tremenda vendetta |
| Give me a day I'll come and kill you. | Di quest'anima è solo desio . . . |
| Men shall see how much I hate you, | Di punirti già l'ora s'affretta, |
| See the vengeance of a clown. | Che fatale per te tuonera. |
| As the lightning shot from Heaven, | Come fulmin scagliato da Dio |
| I will come and strike you down. | Te colpire il buffone saprà. |

**GILDA**

| Oh, my father, your eyes are blazing | O mio padre, qual gioia feroce |
| With a fierce desire for vengeance. | Balenarvi negl'occhi vegg'io! . . . |
| Let me beg you, for my sake save him. | Perdonate . . . a noi pure una voce |
| Oh, my father, my father, forgive. | Di perdono dal cielo verrà. |
| Though he betrayed me, I love him dearly. | (Mi tradiva, pur l'amo, gran Dio, |
| Oh, my father, let him live. | Per l'ingrato ti chiedo pietá!) |

*Curtain.*

*The setting for Act Three in the 1963 production at La Scala. (Teatro alla Scala)*

# Act Three

*A dilapidated riverside bar with a plate-glass window. In front, the road and the river; in the distance, the city. It is night.*\*

**Scene One.** *Gilda and Rigoletto are in the road. / No. 15 Prelude, Scene and Canzone.*

**RIGOLETTO**

You love him?  E l'ami?

**GILDA**

Always.  Sempre.

**RIGOLETTO**

But you've  Pure
Had all this time to recover.  Tempo a guarirne t'ho lasciato.

**GILDA**

I love him.  Io l'amo.

**RIGOLETTO**

Just like a trusting woman. The lying  Povero cor di donna! ... Ah il vile
  coward.    infame! ...
But I'll have my vengeance, Gilda.  Ma avrai vendetta, o Gilda ...

**GILDA**

Oh, not for my sake.  Pietà, mio padre ...

**RIGOLETTO**

And if you were shown for certain  E se tu certa fossi
That he was lying, would you still adore  Ch'ei ti tradisse, l'ameresti ancora?
  him?

**GILDA**

Maybe. I know he loves me.  Nol so, ma pur m'adora.

**RIGOLETTO**

Loves you?  Egli! ...

**GILDA**

Yes.  Sì.

**RIGOLETTO**

Well, then, just wait a moment.  Ebbene, osserva dunque.

†

**GILDA**

      There's someone  Un uomo
Coming!  Vedo!

**RIGOLETTO**

Keep watching closely.  Per poco attendi.

---

\* *A lonely spot on the banks of the River Mincio. On one side stands a house of two storeys that serves as an inn, and in such a dilapidated state, that one can see inside through the half-broken doors and the crevices in the wall. In front, the road and the river; in the distance the city of Mantua.*
*It is night. Sparafucile is cleaning his belt in the inn.*

† (*He leads her to the wall of the inn, and tells her to look through the cracks.*)

65

**Scene Two.** *The Duke, in disguise as a soldier, enters the bar.*

GILDA
*(surprised)*

Oh, father, help me!                                     Ah, padre mio!

DUKE
*(to Sparafucile)*

Come on now. Get moving.                       Due cose, e tosto . . .

SPARAFUCILE

Tell me.                                                      Quali?

DUKE

Bring some wine here, and your sister.       Una stanza e del vino . . .

RIGOLETTO

(His usual directness.)                             (Son questi i suoi costumi!)

SPARAFUCILE

Just as you wish, sir.                                 (Oh il bel zerbino!)
*(He enters the next room.)*

DUKE

| | | |
|---|---|---|
| Women abandon us. | [26] | La donna è mobile |
| Why should it hurt them | | Qual piuma al vento, |
| ıı .. ᵈesert them . . . when it's all over? | | Muta d'accento . . . e di pensiero. |
| Women make fools of us, | | Sempre un amabile |
| Laugh in our faces, | | Leggiadro viso, |
| Cover their traces . . . take a new lover. | | In pianto o in riso . . . e menzognero. |
| Pretty little liars, | | La donna è mobil |
| Cunning little demons – | | Qual piuma al vento, |
| What is a woman? Why should men care? | | Muta d'accento . . . e di pensier. |
| Think of your liberty. | | È sempre misero |
| Those who forget it, | | Chi a lei s'affida, |
| Live to regret it and very badly. | | Chi le confida . . . mal cauto il core! |
| Though we have need of them, | | Pur mai non sentesi |
| Those who confide in them | | Felice appieno |
| Lose all their pride in them, finish up sadly. | | Chi su quel seno . . . non liba amore! |
| Women are liars, | | La donna è mobil |
| Cunning little demons – | | Qual piuma al vento, |
| What is a woman? Why should men care? | | Muta d'accento . . . e di pensier. |

SPARAFUCILE
*(He enters with a bottle of wine and two glasses, which he places on the table.\* The Duke rushes to embrace Maddalena as she enters, but she avoids him. Meanwhile, Sparafucile has gone out on the road and says to Rigoletto:)*

He's here, your rival. Shall I kill him?       È là il vostr'uomo . . . viver dee o morire?
Tell me quickly.

RIGOLETTO

I'll come again and tell you what I want.    Più tardi tornerò l'opra a compire.

*(Sparafucile moves away from the building along the river.)*

**Scene Three.** *Gilda and Rigoletto in the road. Maddalena and the Duke in the bar. / No. 16 Quartet.*

DUKE

When first I came to talk to you    [27]    Un dì, se ben rammentomi,
I thought you very lovely . . .                   O bella, t'incontrai . . .

* *He then beats the ceiling twice with the hilt of his sword. At this signal a pretty young girl, dressed as a gipsy, descends the stairs.*

| | |
|---|---|
| I followed you and asked your name; | Mi piacque di te chiedere |
| You told me that you lived here. | E intesi che qui stai. |
| And from that moment on, | Or sappi, che d'allora |
| Yes, my heart was yours for ever. | Sol te quest'alma adora. |

GILDA

| | |
|---|---|
| You liar! | Iniquo! |

MADDALENA

| | |
|---|---|
| Oh, yes. And all your other women? | Ah, ah!... e vent'altre appresso |
| You must have quite forgotten... | Le scorda forse adesso?... |
| You look the sort of lover | Ha un'aria il signorino |
| Who's had a lot of others. | Da vero libertino... |

DUKE

| | |
|---|---|
| True, I'm such a rogue. | Si?... un mostro son... |

GILDA

| | |
|---|---|
| Oh father help me! | Ah padre mio! |

MADDALENA

| | | | |
|---|---|---|---|
| | Control yourself, | | Lasciatemi. |
| You madman! | | Stordito. | |

DUKE

| | |
|---|---|
| Now what's the matter? | Ih, che fracasso! |

MADDELENA

| | |
|---|---|
| Be patient. | Stia saggio. |

DUKE

| | |
|---|---|
| And you be kind to me, my dear. | E tu sii docile, |
| Don't keep me waiting. | Non fare tanto chiasso. |
| Cast all your inmost fears away. | Ogni saggezza chiudesi |
| Surrender to joy and passion. | Nel gaudio e nell'amore... |

(*He takes her by the hand.*)

| | |
|---|---|
| Your hand is pale and beautiful. | ، La bella mano candida!... |

MADDALENA

| | |
|---|---|
| You're teasing me, you're joking. | Scherzate voi, signore. |

DUKE

| | |
|---|---|
| No, no. | No, no. |

MADDALENA

| | |
|---|---|
| I'm ugly. | Son brutta. |

DUKE

| | |
|---|---|
| Make love to me. | Abbracciami. |

MADDALENA
(*laughing*)

| | |
|---|---|
| Drunkard. | Ebro... |

DUKE

| | |
|---|---|
| I'm drunk with passion. | D'amore ardente. |

MADDALENA

| | |
|---|---|
| You don't know what you're saying. | Signor l'indifferente, |
| Is this some kind of joke?... | Vi piace canzonar?... |

DUKE

| | |
|---|---|
| No, no, I want a wife. | No, no, ti vo'sposar. |

MADDALENA

| | |
|---|---|
| I'll keep you to your promise. | Ne voglio la parola... |

DUKE
(*ironically*)

| | |
|---|---|
| I'm absolutely honest. | Amabile figliuola! |

RIGOLETTO
(*to Gilda, who has seen and understood all*)

| | |
|---|---|
| Is this enough for you? | E non ... ti basta ancor? ... |

GILDA

| | |
|---|---|
| You told me you were true. | Iniquo traditor! |

DUKE

| | |
|---|---|
| If you want a faithful lover, | Bella figlia dell'amore, |
| He is waiting to embrace you. | Schiavo son de' vezzi tuoi |
| You can drive his bitter cares away | Con un detto sol tu puoi |
| And he promises to be true. | Le mie pene consolar. |
| Have some pity. You'll discover | Vieni, e senti del mio core |
| How his heart beats fast for you alone. | Il frequente palpitar. |

MADDALENA

| | |
|---|---|
| You're a lying sort of lover. | Ah! ah! rido ben di core, |
| All these compliments are easy. | Chè tai baie costan poco; |
| If you think you can deceive me | Quanto valga il vostro giuoco, |
| I must tell you I'm no fool. | Mel credete, so apprezzar. |
| Men are easily discovered | Sono avvezza, bel signore, |
| When they do not tell the truth. | Ad un simile scherzare. |

GILDA

| | |
|---|---|
| Oh, I thought you were my lover. | Ah così parlar d'amore |
| How could I believe your lying. | A me pur l'infame ho udito! |
| All my sorrow and my sighing – | Infelice cor tradito, |
| Now my heart will break for you. | Per angoscia non scoppiar. |

RIGOLETTO

| | |
|---|---|
| Softly! You see he is no lover. | Taci, il piangere non vale; |
| Now you know that he was lying. | Ch'ei mentiva sei sicura ... |
| There's no virtue now in crying. | Taci, e mia sarà la cura |
| I will have revenge for you. | La vendetta d'affrettar. |
| Let it come. Let it be fatal. | Sì pronta fia, sarà fatale; |
| I myself will see it through. | Io saprollo fulminar. |

*No. 17 / Scene after the Quartet.*

| | |
|---|---|
| Listen. Go to your home now ... | M'odi, ritorna a casa ... |
| Take some money, pack all your things, | Oro prendi, un destriero, |
| Dress yourself up as a man and leave town. | Una veste viril che t'apprestai, |
| I'll follow you tomorrow ... | E per Verona parti ... |
| Go back to your old home. | Sarovvi io pur doman ... |

GILDA

| | |
|---|---|
| Come with me now ... | Or venite ... |

RIGOLETTO

| | |
|---|---|
| I must stay here. | Impossibil. |

GILDA

| | |
|---|---|
| Help me. | Tremo. |

RIGOLETTO

| | |
|---|---|
| Go. | Va. |

(*Exit Gilda.*)

*During this and the following scene, the Duke and Maddalena talk, laugh and drink. After Gilda's departure Rigoletto goes behind the building, then returns, talking with Sparafucile and giving him money.*

## Scene Four. *Sparafucile, Rigoletto, the Duke and Maddalena.*

**RIGOLETTO**

| | |
|---|---|
| Forty dollars you were asking. Here are twenty. | Venti scudi hai tu detto? . . . Eccone dieci; |
| The rest I'll give you after. | E dopo l'opra il resto |
| He's staying here, then? | Ei qui rimane? |

**SPARAFUCILE**

Yes.                                                      Sì.

**RIGOLETTO**

| | |
|---|---|
| I'll be back at midnight | Alla mezzanotte |
| To take the body. | Ritornerò. |

**SPARAFUCILE**

| | |
|---|---|
| No need to. | Non cale. |
| I'll get rid of him quickly in the river. | A gettarlo nel fiume basto io solo. |

**RIGOLETTO**

No, no, I myself will do it.                    No, no, il vo' far io stesso.

**SPARAFUCILE**

Fine. What's his name?                    Sia . . . il suo nome?

**RIGOLETTO**

| | |
|---|---|
| His and mine go together. | Vuoi saper anche il mio? |
| He is 'Transgression', I am 'Retribution'. | Egli è *Delitto, Punizion* son io. |

*(Exit Rigoletto. It grows dark and thunders.)*

## Scene Five. *Sparafucile, the Duke and Maddalena.*

**SPARAFUCILE**

| | |
|---|---|
| Now the storm's coming closer. | La tempesta è vicina! |
| The night is growing darker. | Più scura fia la notte. |

**DUKE**
*(trying to take hold of her)*

Maddalena!                                        Maddalena? . . .

**MADDALENA**
*(avoiding him)*

| | |
|---|---|
| Wait a moment. If my brother | Aspettate . . . mio fratello |
| Should see us . . . | Viene . . . |

**DUKE**

No problem.                                        Che importa?

**MADDALENA**
*(hearing the thunder)*

Thunder?                                        Tuona?

**SPARAFUCILE**
*(entering)*

It will be raining shortly.                    E pioverà fra poco.

**DUKE**

All the better.                                    Tanto meglio.
*(to Sparafucile)*

| | |
|---|---|
| Why don't you sleep in the outhouse? | Tu dormirai in scuderia . . . |
| Go to blazes. I'll have to stay here. | All'inferno . . . ove vorrai. |

**SPARAFUCILE**

How thoughtful.                                    Grazie.

**MADDALENA**
*(aside to the Duke)*

(For God's sake, leave us.)                    (Ah no . . . partite.)

**DUKE**

(In this weather?)                                          (Con tal tempo?)

**SPARAFUCILE**
(*to Maddalena*)

You'll cost us forty dollars.          Son venti scudi d'oro.
(*to the Duke*)
I'm delighted          Ben felice.
To offer you my bedroom if you would like          D'offrirvi una stanza ... se a voi piace
it.
Come, I will show you up there.          Tosto, a vederla andiamo.
(*He goes to the staircase.*)

**DUKE**

Thank you. I'll follow you. Quickly. Let's          Ebben sono con te ... presto, vediamo.
see it.
(*He whispers a word to Maddalena, and follows Sparafucile.*)

**MADDALENA**

(He's such a young man, handsome and          (Povero giovin! ... grazioso tanto!
friendly.
(*It thunders.*)
Goodness, the air is heavy!)          Dio! ... qual mai notte è questa!)

**DUKE**
(*having been upstairs, and seen the window without shutters*)

You leave the windows open? That's no          Si dorme all'aria aperta? bene, bene ...
problem.
I will take it.          Buona notte.

**SPARAFUCILE**

I wish you pleasant slumbers.          Signor, vi guardi Iddio.

**DUKE**

Let me sleep just a while. I'm quite          Breve sonno dormiam ... stanco son' io.
exhausted.
Women abandon us.          [26] La donna è mobile
Why should it hurt them          Qual piuma al vento,
If we desert them ... When it's all ...          Muta d'accento ... e di pen ...

(*He\* throws himself on the bed, and soon falls asleep. Maddalena downstairs stands sentry near the table, and Sparafucile finishes the bottle left by the Duke. They both remain some time in silence and apparently in deep thought.*)

**MADDALENA**

A good-looking fellow that young man, and          È amabile invero cotal giovinotto.
handsome.

**SPARAFUCILE**

Oh yes, forty dollars is quite a good bargain.          Oh sì, venti scudi ne dà di prodotto.

**MADDALENA**

You're joking. For forty? He's worth so          Sol venti! ... son pochi ... valeva di più.
much more.

**SPARAFUCILE**

Go up there. He's sleeping. Go get me his          La spada,† s'ei dorme, va protami giù.
gun.

(*Maddalena goes upstairs, and admires the sleeping figure. She shades him from the light and returns downstairs.*)

---

\* *puts down his hat and sword, and*
† *literally: 'sword'*

**Scene Six.** *Gilda, disguised as a man, slowly approaches the bar, while Sparafucile continues to drink. Thunder and lightning. / No. 18 Scene, Trio and Storm.*

**GILDA**

| | |
|---|---|
| I cannot think clearly. | Ah più non ragiono! |
| My love brings me back here . . . Oh father, forgive me. | Amor mi trascina? . . . mio padre, perdono . . . |

*(thunder)*

| | |
|---|---|
| The night is so fearful . . . But what will it bring? | Qual notte d'orrore! . . . Gran Dio, che accadrà! |

**MADDALENA**
*(She returns with the Duke's gun.\*)*

| | |
|---|---|
| Just listen. | Fratello? |

**GILDA**
*(looking through the bar window)†*

| | |
|---|---|
| Who said that? | Chi parla? |

**SPARAFUCILE §**

| | |
|---|---|
| Get out of my way. | Al diavol ten va. |

**MADDALENA**

| | |
|---|---|
| He looks like an angel, that guest of ours. I love him. | Somiglia un Apollo quel giovine . . . io l'amo . . . |
| He loves me . . . Don't touch him . . . He's too good to murder. | Ei m'ama . . . riposi . . . nè più l'uccidiamo. |

**GILDA**
*(listening)*

| | |
|---|---|
| To murder! | Oh cielo! . . . |

**SPARAFUCILE**
*(throwing her a sack)*

| | |
|---|---|
| Shut up and get sewing. | Rattoppa quel sacco . . . |

**MADDALENA**

| | |
|---|---|
| But why? | Perchè? |

**SPARAFUCILE**

| | |
|---|---|
| A sack for your angel to bundle him in And throw in the river. | Entr'esso il tuo Apollo, sgozzato da me, Gettar dovrò al fiume. |

**GILDA**

| | |
|---|---|
| He must be the devil! | L'inferno qui vedo! |

**MADDALENA**

| | |
|---|---|
| The question is money. I think we could keep it And still save the young man. | Eppure il danaro salvarti scommetto, Serbandolo in vita. |

**SPARAFUCILE**

| | |
|---|---|
| It's out of the question. | Difficile il credo. |

**MADDALENA**

| | |
|---|---|
| Believe me. There's an easy solution on offer. You already have what the hunchback paid you. He'll come with the rest when the job has been finished. You murder him — | M'ascolta . . . anzi facil ti svelo un progetto. De' scudi, già dieci dal gobbo ne avesti; Venire cogli altri più tardi il vedrai . . . Uccidilo — |

---

\* *sword*
† *looking through a crack in the door*
§ *searching in a cupboard*

71

### GILDA

My father! My father!                          Che sento! Mio padre! . . .

### MADDALENA

—Take all the money that's on him.      —E venti allora ne avrai,
You'll have forty dollars and maybe     Così tutto il prezzo goder si potrà.
some more.

### SPARAFUCILE

Me murder the hunchback? . . . Is that   Uccider quel gobbo! . . . che diavol
what you're saying?                      dicesti!
You think I'm a bandit? I'm some kind    Un ladro son forse? Son forse un
of robber?                               bandito?
Just tell me if ever I've cheated a client.  Qual altro cliente da me fu tradito?
The hunchback engaged me. I'll finish    Mi paga quest'uomo . . . fedele
the job.                                 m'avrà.

### MADDALENA

Oh, show him some mercy!                  Ah grazia per esso.

### SPARAFUCILE

He has to be murdered . . .              È d'uopo ch'ei muoia . . .

### MADDALENA
(*about to go upstairs*)

I'll go up and wake him.                 Fuggire il fo adesso.

### GILDA

She's weeping for him!                   Oh buona figliuola!

### SPARAFUCILE
(*holding her back*)

We'll lose all the money.                Gli scudi perdiamo.

### MADDALENA

That's true! . . .                       È ver! . . .

### SPARAFUCILE

Don't you dare to . . .                  Lascia fare . . .

### MADDALENA

I won't have him murdered.                              Salvarlo dobbiamo.
I won't let him die.                     Salvarlo dobbiamo.

### SPARAFUCILE

I'll leave him alone till the first stroke of   Se pria ch'abbia il mezzo la notte toccato
midnight.                          [31]
If anyone else comes I'll kill him instead.    Alcuno qui giunga, per esso morrà.

### MADDALENA

The night is daunting. The storm will be   È buia la notte, il ciel troppo irato,
breaking.
If nobody comes here my lover is dead.   Nessuno a quest'ora di qui passerà.

### GILDA

Could this be my duty? To die for my     Oh qual tentazione! . . . morir per
lover?                                   l'ingrato! . . .
Oh, father, forgive me! I come here in [32]  Morire! . . . e mio padre! . . . Oh cielo,
dread.                                   pietà!

(*Clocks strike the half hour.*)

### SPARAFUCILE

That leaves thirty minutes.              Ancor c'è mezz'ora.

### MADDALENA
(*weeping*)

Oh, please do not kill him . . .                        Attendi, fratello . . .

72

### GILDA

No, she too is weeping . . . I must go to help him.

Despite all his lies and his heartless behaviour,

I'll sacrifice my life if he can be saved.

Che! piange tal donna! . . . Nè a lui darò aita!

Ah s'egli al mio amore divenne rubello

Io vo' per la sua gettar la mia vita . . .

*(She knocks at the door.)*

### MADDALENA

There's someone.

Si picchia?

### SPARAFUCILE

The wind.

Fu il vento . . .

### MADDALENA
*(Further knocking is heard.)*

There's someone, I tell you.

Si picchia, ti dico.

### SPARAFUCILE

At this time? Who's there?

È strano! Chi è?

### GILDA

I'm down on my luck, sir.
I need food and shelter for one night only.

Pietà d'un mendico;
Asil per la notte a lui concedete.

### MADDALENA

May that night be a long one!

Fia lunga tal notte!

### SPARAFUCILE

Just wait there a moment.

Alquanto attendete.*

### GILDA

Oh Heaven, I beg you, forgive all these sinners!

My life is now over, forgive me this deed.

Oh father, forgive me, I must disobey you.

My lover's in danger . . . I go to save his life.

Ah presso alla morte, sì giovine sono!

Oh cielo per quegl'empi, ti chieggo perdono.

Perdona tu, o padre, a questa infelice! . . .

Sia l'uomo felice . . . ch'or vado a salvar.

### MADDALENA

Come on, get it over. Be quick. Let him in there.

The death of the stranger will save the young man.

Su, spicciati, presto, fa l'opra compita:

Anelo una vita . . . con altra salvar.

### SPARAFUCILE

Alright then, I'm ready. You open the door now.

I'll still get the money. That's all that I want.

Ebbene . . . son pronto, quell'uscio dischiudi;

Più ch'altro gli scudi . . . mi preme salvar.

### MADDALENA

Hurry up.

Spicciàti.

### SPARAFUCILE

Open.

Apri.

### MADDALENA

Come in then.

Entrate.

### GILDA

Heaven, grant them your pardon.

Dio! loro perdonate!

*Maddalena opens the door for Gilda and, in the darkness, Sparafucile knifes her as she enters. The thunder and lightning begin again and then the storm gradually eases.*

---

* He goes to search in the sideboard

**Scene Seven.*** *Rigoletto approaches the bar†. The worst of the storm is over and there are only occasional flashes of lightning and claps of thunder. / Scene after the Trio.*

RIGOLETTO

| | |
|---|---|
| Now for my vengeance, now the moment is ready. | Della vendetta alfin giunge l'istante! |
| Thirty long days I've waited | Da trenta dì l'aspetto |
| In secret sorrow and miserable weeping | Di vivo sangue a lagrime piangendo |
| Playing the fool for all around. | Sotto la larva del buffon . . . Quest'uscio! . . . |

(looking at the bar)

| | |
|---|---|
| He's locked it . . . I'm early . . . There's still a minute left. | E chiuso! . . . Ah non è tempo ancor! . . . S'attenda. |
| How terrible the night is! | Qual notte di mistero! |
| There is a war in Heaven! | Una tempesta in cielo! . . . |
| On earth, on earth a murder! . . . | In terra un omicidio! . . . |
| I understand now what it is to have power! | Oh come invero qui grande mi sento! |

(Midnight strikes.)

| | |
|---|---|
| That was midnight. | Mezzanotte! |

**Scene Eight.** *Enter Sparafucile.*

SPARAFUCILE

| | |
|---|---|
| Who's there? | Chi è la? |

RIGOLETTO
(about to go in)

| | |
|---|---|
| You ready? | Son io. |

SPARAFUCILE

| | |
|---|---|
| I've done it. | Sostate. |

(He leaves and returns dragging a sack.)

| | |
|---|---|
| Here's the man you were wanting. | È qua spento il vostr'uomo . . . |

RIGOLETTO

| | |
|---|---|
| Thank Heaven! Now show me. | Oh gioia! . . . un lume! |

SPARAFUCILE

| | |
|---|---|
| The body? No, where's the money? | Un lume? No, il danaro. |

(Rigoletto gives him the money.)

| | |
|---|---|
| Help me. It's deeper over there. | Lesti all'onda il gettiam . . . |

RIGOLETTO

| | |
|---|---|
| No, I will do it. | No . . . basto io solo. |

SPARAFUCILE

| | |
|---|---|
| It's up to you. Careful where you throw him. | Come vi piace . . . Qui non atto è il sito . . . |
| The water's far too shallow here. Quickly. | Più avanti è più profondo il gorgo . . . Presto |
| Don't let anyone see you. That is all now. | Che alcun non vi sorprenda . . . Buona notte. |

(He re-enters the house.)

**Scene Nine.** *Rigoletto, then the Duke.*

RIGOLETTO

| | |
|---|---|
| This is him, murdered, oh yes, I want to see him! | Egli è là . . . morto! . . . O si . . . vorrei vederlo! |
| Never mind that. I believe it. It has to be him. | Ma che importa! è ben desso! Ecco i suoi sproni! |

---

* *Sparafucile hides behind the door with a knife. Maddalena opens both the outer and inner doors and, while Gilda enters, runs to shut the outer one. Sparafucile shuts the other and everything is silent and dark inside.*

† *closely wrapped in his cloak.*

Oh, if the world could see me . . .
I am the jester. He is the man of power! . . .

Now the jester has crushed him!
I stand here the master . . .
So now I have it, a vengeance for my
  sorrow! . . .
The waves will be his coffin,
His winding-sheet a piece of sacking.
The water, the water!

Ora mi guarda, o mondo . . .
Quest'è un buffone, ed un potente è
  questo! . . .
Ei sta sotto i miei piedi . . .
È desso! oh gioja!
È giunta alfine la tua vendetta, o duolo!

Sia l'onda a lui sepolcro,
Un sacco il suo lenzuolo!
All'onda! all'onda!

(*He tries to drag the sack towards the bank, when he hears the voice of the Duke, crossing the
back of the stage.*)

### DUKE

Women abandon us . . . (*etc.*)

[26] La donna è mobile . . . (*etc.*)

### RIGOLETTO

It's him! It's a mad hallucination . . .

Qual voce! . . . illusion notturna è
  questa! . . .

(*startled*)

No! No! He's alive!

No! . . . no! egli è desso! . . .

(*looking towards the building*)

I have been cheated by you, by you, you
devil!

Maledizione! Olà . . . dimon, bandito?

*No. 20 Scene and Final Duet.*

Then who have I been given? . . .

Chi è mai, chi è qui in sua vece! . . .

(*opening the sack*)

I'm trembling. A human body! . . .

Io tremo . . . È umano corpo! . . .

(*The sky lightens.*)

**The last scene.** *Rigoletto and Gilda.*

### RIGOLETTO

My daughter! . . . Gilda, my daughter! . . .
Oh no . . . it's not her, she has left the
  city . . .

Mia figlia! . . . Dio! . . . mia figlia! . . .
Ah no . . . è impossibil! . . . per Verona è in
  via!

(*kneeling*)

I'm going mad! It is her!
Oh my Gilda, my darling, oh, please say
something!

Fu vision! . . . È dessa! . . .
Oh mia Gilda! . . . fanciulla a me
rispondi! . . .

(*He knocks desperately at the door.*)

Tell me who can have done this . . .
Come out! They've tricked me.
It's locked. My daughter,
My Gilda, oh my daughter!

L'assassino mi svela . . .
Olà . . . Nessuno!
Nessun! . . . mia figlia? . . .
Mia Gilda! oh mia figlia?

### GILDA

Who is calling?

Chi mi chiama?

### RIGOLETTO

She's talking. She's not dead.
She's breathing. Oh Heaven!
Oh the one possession left to me!
She's breathing, she seems to know me.

Ella parla! si move!
È viva! oh Dio!
Ah mio ben solo in terra
Mi guarda . . . mi conosci.

### GILDA

Oh dearest father!

Ah padre mio!

### RIGOLETTO

What has happened? My child,
Have you been wounded? Tell me—

Qual mistero! che fu!
Sei tu ferita? dimmi—

### GILDA
(*pointing to her heart*)

It's here, here, here, I've been stabbed.

L'acciar qui, qui mi piagò.

**RIGOLETTO**

| | |
|---|---|
| Who could have done this? | Chi t'ha colpita? |

**GILDA**

| | |
|---|---|
| It's all my fault. I tried to deceive you. | V'ho ingannato . . . colpevole fui . . . |
| But I loved him. Now I'm dying for him. | L'amai troppo . . . ora muoio per lui! |

**RIGOLETTO**
*(to himself)*

| | |
|---|---|
| God of vengeance, she was caught by the arrow, | Dio tremendo! Ella stessa fu colta |
| By the arrow that I shot at my enemy. | Dallo stral di mia giusta vendetta! |

*(to Gilda)*

| | |
|---|---|
| Dearest angel, come, look at your father. | Angiol cara mi guarda, m'ascolta. |
| Speak, oh, speak to me, Gilda, my daughter! | Parla, parlami, figlia diletta! |

**GILDA**

| | |
|---|---|
| Oh let me rest now! For me, for my sake, forgive him. | Ah ch'io taccia! a me, a lui perdonate! |
| I'm your daughter, give your blessing, oh my father. | Benedite alla figlia o mio padre . . . |

[33]

| | |
|---|---|
| Ah, soon, in Heaven, when I'm near to my mother, | Lassù in cielo, vicina alla madre |
| I'll pray the Lord for a blessing on you. | In eterno per voi pregherò. |

**RIGOLETTO**

| | |
|---|---|
| You must not die. You're my angel, my treasure. | Non morir mio tersoro pietàde, |
| Pity your father, don't leave me alone. | Mia colomba, lasciarmi non dei, |
| If you go, I have no-one, I have nothing on earth. | Se t'involi, qui sol, qui sol rimarei, |
| If you die, I must die here with you. | Non morire o qui teco morrò! |

**GILDA**

| | |
|---|---|
| No more. Forgive him, my father. | Non più. A lui perdonate, mio padre. |
| Farewell now. | Addio. |

*(She dies.)*

**RIGOLETTO**

| | |
|---|---|
| Gilda, my Gilda, she's murdered! | Gilda! mia Gilda! È morta! |
| Ah, ah, the old man cursed me! | Ah! la maledizione! |

*(He collapses in despair\* beside his daughter's body.)*

*Final Curtain.*

---

\* *tearing his hair*

**Discography** /*Martin Hoyle* All complete versions are in stereo and in Italian. For detailed analysis and comparison the enthusiast is referred to *Opera on Record* (ed. Alan Blyth, Hutchinson, 1979).

| Conductor | *Serafin* | *Sanzogno* | *Solti* | *Bonynge* | *Molinari-Pradelli* |
|---|---|---|---|---|---|
| Company/Orchestra | **La Scala, Milan** | **Sta Cecilia** | **RCA Italiana** | **Ambrosian Singers, LSO** | **Dresden State Opera, Staatskapelle** |
| *Rigoletto* | Gobbi | MacNeil | Merrill | Milnes | Panerai |
| *Duke* | Di Stefano | Cioni | Kraus | Pavarotti | Bonisolli |
| *Gilda* | Callas | Sutherland | Moffo | Sutherland | Rinaldi |
| *Sparafucile* | Zaccaria | Siepi | Flagello | Talvela | Rundgren |
| *Maddalena* | Lazzarini | Malagù | Elias | Tourangeau | Cortez |
| | | | | | |
| Disc UK number | SLS5018 | GOS 655-7 | RL42865 | SET 542-4 | HA 21474 |
| Tape UK number | TC-SLS5018 | | | K2A3 | |
| Excerpts (Disc) | | | | SET580 | |
| Excerpts (Tape) | | | | CET580 | |
| Disc US number | Angel 353CL | LON 1322 | LSC7027 | 13105 | |
| Tape US number | | | | 5-13105 | |
| Excerpts (Disc) US | | | LSC2837 | 26401 | |
| Excerpts (Tape) US | | | RK1050 | 5-26401 | |

| Conductor | Rudel | Giulini | Molinari-Pradelli | Kubelik |
|---|---|---|---|---|
| Company/Orchestra | Ambrosian Singers, Philharmonia | Vienna State Opera, VPO | San Carlo, Naples | La Scala, Milan |
| Rigoletto | Milnes | Cappuccilli | Capecchi | Fischer-Dieskau |
| Duke | Kraus | Domingo | Tucker | Bergonzi |
| Gilda | Sills | Cotrubas | D'Angelo | Scotto |
| Sparafucile | Ramey | Ghiaurov | Sardi | |
| Maddalena | Dunn | Obraztsova | Pirazzini | Cossotto |
| Disc UK number | SLS5193 | 2740 225 | 6747 407 | 2709 014 |
| Tape UK number | 3371 054 | | 3371 001 | |
| Excerpts (Disc) | | 2537 057 | | |
| Excerpts (Tape) | 3306 057 | | | |
| Disc US number | SZX3872 | 2740 225 | 6770016 | 2709 014 |
| Tape US number | 3371 054 | 3371 054 | 7650016 | 3371 001 |
| Excerpts (Disc) US | | 2537 057 | | |
| Excerpts (tape) US | | | | 922 017 |

**Excerpts** Of necessity, the following list provides a sample only of the immense recorded corpus of material from this opera. The specialised collector is again referred to *Opera on Record* for more detailed and comprehensive information.

| Number | Artist | Disc | Tape |
|---|---|---|---|
| *Questa o quella* | McCormack | SH399 | TC-SH399 |
| " | Schipa | GEMM192 | |
| " | Burke | VIP104 | |
| " | Fernandi | | TCT-MOM120 |
| " | Wunderlich (*in German*) | 300356 | |
| " | Bergonzi | 6570045 | |
| " | Domingo | ARL10048 | |
| " | Pavarotti | D236D2 | K236K22 |
| " | Bonisolli | DC23068 | |
| *È il sol dell'anima* (love duet) | Callas, Di Stefano | SLS856 | |
| *Caro nome* | Berger (*in German*) | RL30439 | |
| " | Callas | SLS5104 | TC-SLS5104 |
| " | Sutherland | SXL6193 | |
| " | Grist | | TC2-MOM120 |
| " | Cotrubas | 76521 | |
| " | Barrientos | C0403 | |
| *Ella mi fu rapita* | Nash | GEMM210 | |
| " | Pavarotti | D253D2 | K253K22 |
| " | Bonisolli | DC23068 | |
| *Cortigiani* | Schlusnus (*in German*) | RL30439 | |
| " | Bruson | SDD570 | |
| *La donna è mobile* | McCormack | SH399 | TC-SH399 |
| " | Pavarotti | D253D2 | K253K22 |
| " | Caruso | RK11749 | |
| " | Aragall | DC29391 | |
| " | Schipa | GEMM192 | |
| " | Burke | VIP104 | |
| " | Fernandi | | TC-MOM120 |
| " | Wunderlich | 300356 | |
| " | Bergonzi | 6570 045 | |
| " | Bonisolli | DC23068 | |
| *Bella figlia dell' amore* (quartet) | Melba, Thornton, McCormack, Sammarco | SH399 | TC-SH399 |
| " | Talley, Gordon, Gigli, De Luca | GEMM 202-6 | |
| " | Grist, Di Stasio, Gedda, MacNeil | | TC2-MOM120 |
| *Various selections* | Caruso, Abott, *etc.* | GV536 | |
| " | Björling, Peters, *etc.* | RL43243 | RK43243 |
| " | Gyurkovics, Tiszay, Kenez, Simandy, Sved, Szekely | LPX12344 | |

# Bibliography

The opera is the last chapter in the first volume of Julian Budden's superb 3-volume study *The Operas of Verdi* (Cassell, 1973). Classic biographies remain Frank Walker's extraordinary *The Man Verdi* (London, 1962) and Francis Toye's *Giuseppe Verdi: His Life and Works* (London, 1931). Roger Parker translated and edited Gabriele Baldini's *The Story of Giuseppe Verdi* (Cambridge, 1980) an unconventional and exciting book; David R.B. Kimbell's *Verdi in the Age of Romanticism* (Cambridge, 1981) contains much fascinating background material which other studies do not touch. Vincent Godefroy discusses the opera in *The Dramatic Genius of Verdi* (Volume I) (London, 1975) and there are relevant source texts in William Weaver's lavishly illustrated *Verdi: A Documentary Study* (Thames & Hudson, 1977). Charles Osborne's edition of the Verdi letters (Gollancz, 1971) is the only one available in English.

Victor Hugo's *Le Roi s'amuse* is not readily available in English.

*Young Romantics* by Linda Kelly (Bodley Head, 1976) and *Sublime and Grotesque: A Study of French Romantic Drama* by W.D. Howarth (Harrap, 1975) are two excellent books about the 19th century French Romantic theatre.

# Contributors

Jonathan Keates teaches English at the City of London School, and is currently working on a biography of Handel.

Roger Parker is Assistant Professor of Music at Cornell University.

Peter Nichols, Rome Correspondent of *The Times*, is the author of many books about Italy including *Italia! Italia!* and *The Pope's Divisions*.

James Fenton is drama critic of *The Sunday Times* and has published a collection of his poems *The Memory of War* (Salamander, 1982).